A CHRISTIAN
THEOLOGY OF
EDUCATION

A
CHRISTIAN THEOLOGY
OF
EDUCATION

Rupert E. Davies

*(Formerly Chaplain of Kingswood School, Bath,
and Principal of Wesley College, Bristol)*

DENHOLM HOUSE PRESS
Robert Denholm House,
Nutfield, Surrey RH1 4HW

F
29
206

First published 1974
© Rupert E. Davies 1974
ISBN 0 85213 096 1

To my family, all members of which,
whether they know it or not, are teachers.

Printed in Hungary by the
ALFÖLDI PRINTING HOUSE, DEBRECEN

115770

CONTENTS

Bible quotations are from the
New English Bible

by

*Professor W. R. Niblett C.B.E., B.A., B.Litt.,
formerly Dean of the University of London
Institute of Education*

Why do Christian teachers need a theology of education at all? Is it not asking too much to suggest that they should be able to think theologically as well as educationally about the subjects they are teaching? Couldn't they just accept the corpus of Christian doctrine and then apply it to the best of their ability? The answers to such questions are not simple, but Mr. Davies's book is a great help to thought about them. To take an example of the difficulties: reference to "the corpus of Christian Doctrine" conveys the impression that there is one way, and one way only, of stating the main truths of Christianity, that its insights and message are to be expressed in the same terms down the ages—irrespective of the century and society in which the Christian lives and the stage of maturity he has reached. In other words, that theological knowledge is cognitive and objective knowledge only, and that theological *perception*—in Christian language the working within the individual understanding of the Holy Spirit—is unimportant. But Christian truth is in continuing revelation.

Over the centuries more and more of the social and educational consequences of holding a Christian position have become clear—to a few men first, then to larger numbers. The incompatibility, now almost universally acknowledged, of Christianity and slavery was felt by relatively few even in the west 250 years ago. Today whether or not it is Christian to encourage Jews or Moslems or Buddhists to worship in their own way can give rise to intense discussion. Views still differ sharply whether it is justifiable to lease or sell a building which has been a Christian church to a congregation of some non-Christian faith. One's judgement in such cases will be informed by what one conceives to be implied not only by a Christian morality, but also by a Christian concept of God.

Such matters are not for the Religious Education period alone (where R.E. would still exist as a separate subject and has not itself become assimilated into "Integrated Humanities"). Christian teachers of history or science or English or art or geography need an adequate Christian theology of education not only because of the secular presuppositions which so often are quietly but profoundly embodied in the subject they are teaching, but because they may be as well in charge of forms, houses and out of school activities.

Mr. Davies's book is not an easy one, nor did the author intend it to be. There is much learning in it, philosophic as well as Biblical knowledge, and, as the later parts witness, he draws on great experience of the classroom and the school. One may of course challenge or not accept, at any rate at first, some of his statements, even his theological statements. But I suspect that he would not have that otherwise; for such a challenge and questioning will only come from the reader of lively mind—the one for whom he is, in particular, catering. His own orthodoxy is never of a kind that is secondhand: it has been personally won. He does not conceal his personal faith. But, as he well knows, faith is no substitute for the hard thinking which theology demands. This book is a facilitating environment in which theological thought, a Christian theology of education, and an individual faith may grow.

ROY NIBLETT

Introductory Note

This is not a theology of Religious Education, but, if it is anything, a Christian theology of education. This needs to be made clear at the start, since it is sadly customary for Christian writers to devote all their attention to Religious Education in the sense of the Bible period and the school's daily worship.

There is here not even a chapter on Religious Education, in this sense, partly to destroy the suspicion that the author, despite his protestations, is really beguiling the reader to continue till he reaches the climax, which turns out to be a chapter on Religious Education after all. But there *is* a discussion of Religious Education in the last chapter within the context of education in general, since to leave it out would rudely disrupt the argument of the book.

It could perhaps be said that the first chapter is designed to persuade non-teacher Christians of the Christian significance of education, and that the second chapter is designed to persuade teachers of all sorts of the educational significance of theology. But both these chapters are essential to the whole, and the difference is merely one of emphasis. No such distinction of aim or emphasis should be looked for in the remaining chapters.

I willingly acknowledge my debt to Douglas Hubery, General Secretary of the Division of Education and Youth of the Methodist Church, who urged me on to write this book, and to his book *Christian Education in State and Church* (Denholm House Press, 1972); to Kenneth Wilson, formerly Chaplain of Kingswood School, Bath, now tutor at Wesley College, Bristol, for his advice; and to my publishers, for taking such a risk.

Bristol, 1974   RUPERT E. DAVIES

1

The Palindrome of Revelation

When the carefully selected and highly trained athletes of the ancient Greek cities competed in the 'stadion', the foot-race, at the Olympic Games, each of them, at the starter's command, ran the course of 210 yards up to a pole assigned to him, then round the pole and back to his starting point. This rapid doubling-back must have involved a technique hard to acquire, and scarcely conducive to a time for the race which we should put in the record-breaking class. But a man who completed this there-and-back-again course more speedily than the other competitors was entitled to a crown of wild-olive, a palm-branch, public entertainment in the Civic Hall for the rest of his life (if he was an Athenian), the right to a place in battle near the king (if he was a Spartan) and, if he happened to live in the first half of the fifth century B.C., to a celebratory ode by the immortal poet, Pindar.

Thus the ancient Olympic '400 metres' was palindromic: its starting-point and its finishing-point were identical. Perhaps it is from this fact that the meaning of the word 'palindrome' is derived: 'a word or verse that reads the same backwards as forwards'—such as 'radar'. Probably the most famous example of this phenomenon is the very complicated and somewhat

9

mysterious 'Corinium acrostic' found near Cirencester in which the five Latin words read equally well from right to left and left to right, from bottom to top and top to bottom. As the words used are made up of all the letters of 'Pater Noster', the acrostic is probably a secret Christian sign from the years of imperial persecution.[1]

But a deeper significance can be read into it. Like the 'stadion' at Olympia, it points, albeit no doubt unconsciously, to the nature of divine revelation as Christians may understand it. Of every period in Christian history it can be said, in Tennyson's words, that 'all day long the noise of battle raged' between those who identify, virtually or explicitly, God's revelation of himself with the human quest for truth, so that the Bible becomes a record of human spiritual and intellectual effort; and those who insist that human enquiry is nothing to the point, because God has revealed himself without the aid of man as largely as he intends to do, and has done so plainly, with the result that all that man has to do is to accept the revelation proffered to him by God. The Schoolmen suggested a kind of middle way between these extremes, according to which man reaches a large measure of truth by means of his own capacity for knowledge (itself, of course, a gift of God), and is then granted supernatural knowledge.

The 'middle way' was in its turn denounced by the Reformation theologians as setting too high a store by reason. The pendulum swung back in the Age of Reason, not least among the English Deists, who thought of revelation as merely confirming what reason had already disclosed. Karl Barth initiated a violent reaction, and the air was thick with denun-

10

ciations of those who clung to the idea that there was any vestige of 'natural' theology at all.

But now it may be possible to transcend this gloomy polarization. In the Olympic 'stadion' the starting point and the finishing point were the same, and the same distance was traversed twice in two directions. In something of the same way, God is the source of truth, and so is the starting-point of all revelation. Therefore no truth is known unless he reveals it, whether it be truth about the natural order, or truth about ultimate reality. He is also the finishing point of all revelation, since all knowledge, truly so called, is knowledge of truth, and all truth is revealed by God, and it is to God we come by seeking for the truth. The course was not completed at Olympia unless the runner himself turned back in his tracks and reached the point from which he had started. Similarly, revelation remains purely abstract unless those to whom it is offered themselves turn towards the source of that revelation and battle their way towards it until they reach it.

But this must be put into less symbolic terms, no doubt, if it is to carry conviction, since, like all other analogies, this one fails to fit the situation precisely.

So let us put the matter in this way. God is the source and origin of our understanding of the natural world. It is his mind in which the ordering of the visible universe is conceived and from which what we call the laws of nature are derived. It is his purposes which all created things serve according to their constitution and their dynamism. The principles of logic and mathematics, in conformity with which creation is for ever taking place, are the ways of his thinking and planning. It is in his all-embracing, wholly consistent design that all the sometimes obviously

11

harmonious, sometimes apparently contradictory processes, progressions and retrogressions of nature find their ultimate unity. It is by his will and power that things are as they are, change as they change, are fulfilled as they are fulfilled, finish as they finish. He is the creator, since without his will nothing exists, and by his will everything that exists has its existence; he is the designer, since it is according to his thought that all things belong together and serve their proper ends. He is the illuminator, since without his provision no knowledge would be possible, and it is by his enlightenment of our minds that we know what we know and think as we think.

But it does not strike us that way as enquiring human beings—at least, not immediately and often not at all. We start with the world as we find it and with ourselves as we find ourselves, with the thinking apparatus with which we are endowed; and slowly, tentatively, painfully, we ask questions and make experiments, and amass a body of information which we trust in so far as it helps us to go further into the subject we are investigating. And out of the miscellanies of fact and theory there seems to emerge an orderly outline, and even the faint glimmerings of a design, and even of a purpose, until sometimes, in fact quite often, as the climax of centuries or decades of trial and error, a theory is formulated, confirmed and elaborated and then made the basis of other theories later to be created.

All this takes place without any conscious reference to God, of any sort whatever. In fact, it can well be maintained that to think of God during the accumulation of scientific knowledge would cloud the issue or fudge the facts; at best it would confuse two things which need to be distinguished, the facts themselves and their ultimate interpretation.

God is the source and origin of human existence. Our bodily and mental structures are formed according to his specification; they are not the result of a series of accidental conjunctions. Our aims and ideals are coherent and significant within the framework of his purposes for the universe. Our ethical judgements are adumbrations, however dim, of his goodness, and of his judgement on evil. Our aspirations are towards his holiness and purity; our guilt, and even our despair of goodness, are unconscious recognitions of his claims upon us. He is love, and human love is the effluence of the divine love. He is beauty, and the beautiful objects which we make are reflections of the divine splendour.

But this is not how psychologists, anthropologists, biologists, sociologists and creative artists view the matter. To them human existence is the object of scientific enquiry; and art is the product of the human genius. And their attitude is impeccable. For man to understand himself and his fellows, in his personal nature and in his social relationships, a religious hypothesis formulated in advance of the discovery of the facts is a dangerous encumbrance. So human emotions, conations and relationships must be looked at without any preconceptions, philosophical or religious, anti-philosophical or anti-religious. It is notorious that the proper study of man became possible, and capable of steady advance, only when the dogmas of God's image in man and of original sin ceased to dominate psychological study—indeed, only when these dogmas ceased to play any part in the whole enquiry (this fact does not in any sense contradict the view that God's image *is* in man, or that man *is* guilty of original sin!). It is equally notorious that, although art as expressive of religious emotion is as authentically a form of art as any other form, any prescription to any artist that his work must reflect a relationship to God, friendly *or* hostile, cramps his style and invalidates his activity—in fact, it probably puts him out of business as an artist altogether and reduces him to the status of a propagandist or imitator.

Nor do religiously prescribed ethics fare any better. The problems of moral choice and the formulation of ethical principles constitute a philosophical subject which is necessarily autonomous so far as its premisses, hypotheses and methods are concerned. The ultimate reference of ethical decisions is for the ethical philosopher a matter of open enquiry, whatever his conclusions, theistic or non-theistic, turn out to be.

This brings us to philosophy in the general sense. God is the ground of all knowledge and truth. The famous Oxford lines about Benjamin Jowett were not true of Jowett, but they *are* true of God:

What there is to know, I know it;

. . . .

What I don't know isn't knowledge.

The ultimate definition of truth has to be: truth is what God knows; though the definition cannot be acceptable to anyone who does not believe in God or cannot see any meaning in the word 'God'. We are assuming, of course, both that 'God' is a meaningful word and that God exists; this is not the place to argue those particular propositions. On these assumptions it must be that only in God is undeniable truth to be found, and that in God the whole truth resides.

14

But this is not how the matter seems to the philosopher to stand—at least, if he is a modern philosopher. When it was thought possible to demonstrate the existence of God as a necessary truth, philosophers did indeed look at the matter almost in the way which the last paragraph described; and such a view of the matter gives to the Schoolmen the particular quality of dogmatism which alienates us from them. But is has long since been shown by Kant and others that the existence of God cannot be shown to be a necessary truth, since the ontological argument, with all others purporting to prove the existence of God, lacks cogency. Nor indeed does the Christian theologian rely on the Kantian arguments alone to disprove the demonstrability of God's existence. He argues also that if God could be proved to exist, his existence could not be in doubt for any man in possession of ordinary human reason; in other words, no rational being would be free to doubt his existence. But it is of the essence of the Christian conception of God that he is held always to leave man the freedom to doubt and deny the truth, as well as to disobey the divine law. So if God could be proved to exist, the God thus demonstrated would not be the God of the Christian revelation.

So no one needs shed any tears that the existence of God cannot be proved. Freed from the cumpulsion to accept the necessary existence of God, post-Kantian philosophers have gone off in so many different directions that it is hard to define the task of philosophy in any way acceptable to all those who pursue it. But it is of course true to say of them all that, as philosophers, they would totally reject the notion that they should accept the absolute priority of God as a premiss to their arguments, for God is for them, and must be, an open question. The Hegelians, German and British, tended to suppose that they had demonstrated the existence of the Absolute, and the Absolute can be identified with God; yet this was an inference from the nature and work of the human mind, and in their thought it is, in fact, mind which has the priority once ascribed to God. F. H. Bradley, it is true, flinches from the conclusion that reality is purely rational and that existence is the same as understanding: 'that the glory of the world in the end is appearance leaves the world more glorious, if we feel it is a show of some fuller splendour; but the sensuous curtain is a deception and a cheat, if it hides some colourless movement of atoms, some spectral woof of impalpable abstractions, or unearthly ballet of bloodless categories. Though dragged to such conclusions, we cannot embrace them. Our principles may be true, but they are not reality. They no more *make* that whole which commands our devotion, than some shredded dissection of human tatters *is* that warm and breathing beauty of flesh which our hearts found delightful'.

But Bradley does not relinquish his adherence to the conviction that 'the desire to comprehend our Universe as the double outgrowth and revelation of a single principle, depends on a genuine impulse of philosophy'.[2] So for the Idealists, of whom Bradley was surely the outstanding British example, the discovery of reality is the result of a quest, not of a revelation.

Of philosophers in the empiricist tradition, from Aristotle onwards, this can be stated with even greater assurance. 'Nothing is in the intellect which was not previously in the senses' is a principle which

16

disallows any method of approach to truth except through human experience of the physical world. Empiricists are not notable for reaching God at the end of their chain of reasoning, though Aristotle did do exactly that; but they certainly reject any possibility that God can be reached in any other way.

Some schools of modern empiricism have pushed the matter even further. They have used the Verification Principle—that no statement has meaning which cannot be verified or falsified, that is, have all rational doubt about it removed, by experience derived from the senses—as a starting point for all philosophical discussion. They have thus quickly concluded that since the existence of God can be neither verified nor falsified the statement that he exists is meaningless. Thus, for the Logical Positivist, enquiry into God is not only a quest, but a hopeless quest. The weakness of this view, often pointed out, is that the Verification Principle is itself incapable of verification, and is, therefore, presumably meaningless. Yet it is used, for the purpose of dismissing theology, as dogmatically as the existence of God was once used for dismissing doubt. The Linguistic Philosophers who followed hard upon the Logical Positivists did not repeat this error, and have in no case discounted the possibility that God-language may refer to an existent being. In any case, it may even be that the day of the anti-metaphysicians is almost over, and we may soon find students reading Hegel and Bradley again, no doubt shamefacedly in some corner which they hope to keep unobserved.[3] But for all these philosophers, metaphysical and empiricist alike, philosophy is an enquiry, not a revelation.

The double action of divine revelation and human

enquiry which we have discovered in the main fields of human knowledge is exemplified even in the Bible itself, which is normally and rightly thought of above all as an instrument of divine revelation. Liberal theologians of the first quarter of this century did, indeed, describe the Bible as the story of man's quest for God, and the manifest inaccuracy of this description provoked a violent reaction from the neo-orthodox of the Barthian and semi-Barthian schools of thought. This reached its climax in the many-volumed works of Anders Nygren, *Agape and Eros*,[4] where he maintained, with a wealth of evidence from Biblical and historical sources, that on the Christian view *Eros,* that is, man's longing after God and search for him, is in essence egocentric, or at least anthropocentric, and bound to fail; while *Agape,* which is primarily God's outgoing love to man, provides all that man needs in the way of salvation and truth without any effort on his part, save that of appropriating what is offered to him.

It is possible now to see fairly clearly the error in the liberal way of describing the Bible. It is a serious error, no doubt, but it is an error of emphasis rather than of substance. The Bible, without question, portrays God as the sole fountain of truth and righteousness and love, and it is his word alone which from the creation to the consummation of all things enlightens man's ignorance and dispels his errors. In the beginning, God ... 'My thoughts are not your thoughts, and your ways are not my ways. This is the very word of the Lord. For as the heavens are higher than the earth, so are my ways higher than your ways and my thoughts than your thoughts; and as the rain and the snow come down from heaven and do not return until they have watered the earth, making it blossom and bear fruit, and give seed for sowing and bread to eat, so shall the word which comes from my mouth prevail; it shall not return to me fruitless, without accomplishing my purpose or succeeding in the task I gave it.'[5] 'For the same God who said, "Out of darkness let light shine", has caused his light to shine within us, to give the light of revelation—the revelation of the glory of God in the face of Jesus Christ.'[6] These are not isolated passages; they express the *leitmotif* of both Old and New Testaments when they speak of God's relationship to ignorant and sinful humanity. So far Nygren was right.

But there is another strain in Biblical thought, often recessive, never dominant, but, equally, never entirely absent—the never-ceasing search of man for God. 'Inquire of the Lord while he is present, call upon him when he is close at hand' is from the same portion of the writings of the Second Isaiah as the earlier Isaianic quotation.[7] This strain of ideas is especially prominent in the Book of Job, which is admittedly somewhat out of the mainstream of Old Testament thought: 'If only I knew how to find him, how to enter his court, I would state my case before him and set out my arguments in full; then I should learn what answer he would give and find out what he had to say'.[8] In the concluding chapters of the book God does give Job his answer, out of the whirlwind and somewhat wrathfully, but an answer none the less.[9] Jesus says: 'Ask, and you will receive; seek, and you will find; knock, and the door will be opened. For everyone who asks receives, he who seeks finds, and to him who knocks, the door will be opened'.[10] And this is St. Paul at Athens, as Luke conceives him to have spoken: 'He created every race of men of one stock, to inhabit the whole earth's surface ... They were to seek God, and, it might be, touch and find him; though indeed he is not far from each of us, for in him we live and move, and in him we exist'.[11]

Pascal speaks of God as saying to us: 'Comfort yourself, you would not seek me if you had not found me',[12] and we might well reply: 'We should not have sought for you if you had not already found us'. But it is also to be said that the men of the Bible who seek for God in unawareness of God's already-given revelation receive approval rather than disapproval from the Biblical writers, and are certainly never instructed to give up searching on the ground that their searching will lead them nowhere.

We have now, it is to be hoped, established the fact that in the principal areas of human enquiry—those covered by the natural and human sciences, the study of ethics, and the philosophical investigation of reality—there is, in the Christian view, a two-way traffic. God is believed to be the source and beginning of truth and knowledge, man conceives himself to be discovering the truth for himself. But at this point it is necessary to indicate that although the traffic is two-way, yet it is not for all stages of the journey on the same road; there is quite a complex of one-way streets, and sometimes the road from God to man goes through different country from that traversed by the road from man to God. In general, the road from man to God, the road of human enquiry, is much more tortuous and circuitous than the road from God to man (though it is not to be supposed that the road from God to man is itself undeviatingly straight for all its course). For while God's revelation of himself to man is

20

directed by God himself and is held up only by the ignorance of man and the barriers which man erects, man's enquiry into truth is directed by man, in his weakness as well as in his strength, and leads him up many culs-de-sac which are not plainly indicated before they are entered, and sends him round many detours which an omnicompetent engineer would have avoided.

Most seriously of all, man's search for truth, however prolonged, however carefully planned and carried out, can and does often go astray, or fall short of reaching its destination, and when it does reach its destination it leaves the searcher still uncertain whether he has reached his destination or not—just as the car-driver in war-time England, when the signposts were removed, could never be sure if he was on the right road, and when he reached a town was not sure whether the town he was in was the one he had been aiming at.

This point needs further explanation. It is of the essence of scientific enquiry into the physical world and the nature of man that in the end it is brought up short. There are frontiers which it cannot and does not wish to cross. Granted the laws of thermodynamics, granted the theory of relativity in its most sophisticated form, granted the truth of evolutionary theory as it is now developing—what then? That question 'what then?' takes a different form according to the subject under discussion, but in each case it is unanswerable in the terms of the science from which it is derived. What is the meaning and purpose of the thermo-nuclear structure of the universe? Indeed, has it any meaning or purpose? Man has reached his present stage of development by the process which we can approximately describe: is this by chance, or by the will and activity of a creator? Man's thought and intentions and actions can be shown to have a place in a cause-and-effect process whose past can be mapped out and whose future can be predicted: what meaning has 'freedom' in this context, if it has any meaning at all? And so on.

The results of ethical reflexion are different, though equally problematic. C. D. Broad, in a famous book, distinguished seven types of ethical theory, and most writers would acknowledge that this number is approximately right. But no ethical philosopher would come down in a wholly convinced way on the side of one of these seven—though he may well claim to have disproved the majority of the seven.

In general philosophy the variety is considerably greater, and though there are various schools of thought which have from time to time done battle with passionate intensity, no member of any school claims to have disposed of his opponents definitively. In fact, the very intensity of the passion displayed points, as in other areas of life, to uncertainty in the minds of the contestants. It is true that Hegel spoke and lived as if he had mastered all the major secrets of the universe, but the subsequent collapse of his system has warned his successors off such arrogance. A. J. Ayer, in his comparative youth, claimed in *Language, Truth and Logic*[13] to have provided solutions of the major problems of philosophy in the first seven chapters, and of the minor ones in the eighth and last one; but no doubt he has subsequently repented of this attitude.[14] Behaviourist psychologists sometimes profess to have demonstrated a system of rigid determinism in human action, but this is because they are oblivious of the fact that by asserting their view to be true—which they certainly do assert—they are themselves contradicting those views; for if we are all rigidly determined, so are they, and the claim to *truth,* anywhere and everywhere, collapses. In the same way, Bertrand Russell from time to time claimed to have demonstrated the meaninglessness of life—and thereby asserted the meaninglessness of his own view.

Thus human enquiry leads us not to answers, but to questions. But, we may say with fair confidence, to the *right* questions. The sciences and the philosophies, ethical and other, have conducted an extensive and an extensively effective cleaning-up campaign; superstition, in its broadest sense, religious and secular, is on its way to complete elimination; there are many questions that we now know it would be foolish to ask, answers that we know that we can no longer give. The proof of man's late emergence on the terrestrial scene, of the immensity of the universe, of the atomic structure of physical reality, of the ambiguity of the word 'freedom', of the psychosomatic character of human pleasure and pain—these and many other similar things have opened the mind to vistas of truth which were previously shrouded in fitful darkness.

The fundamental relationship of divine revelation to human enquiry is that the revelation propounds the answers to the questions posed by the enquiry. The answers given by the revelation are 'theological' answers. This does not mean that they are couched in theological terms or conform to any theological viewpoint. It means that they relate to the total human situation, which, in the Christian view, is *coram Deo;* all human life is lived in the presence of God, and is related to him at all points, knowingly or not. This is the sense in which it is true to say that

23

God is both the starting-point of revelation and the finishing-point of human inquiry. In the last resort man, when he finds the truth, finds the truth of God; and without God's revelation this point would never have been reached. And this is still the case whether or not at the end of the enquiry the enquirer is an atheist or a theist.

With these considerations in mind, we can try to make good the claim that the long-established polarity of revelation and reason, natural and revealed theology, can be overcome. We must first look a little more closely at the polarity, and amplify our previous description.

It is agreed that natural theology may be defined as man's knowledge of God acquired without the assistance of revelation—chiefly by reason, but also by artistic imagination and ethical insight; while revealed theology is man's knowledge of God given by divine revelation. The Schoolmen in general, as we have seen, asserted the existence and value of natural theology, though William of Occam, at the end of the long series of theologian philosophers, was so impressed by the 'contradictions' of human reason that he came near to abandoning all faith in it. They went on to say that natural theology, though reliable within its limits (the limits being variously drawn by individual thinkers), was insufficient, and both needed and received completion from revealed theology. Grace does not abolish nature—it completes it; divine revelation does not cancel human reason—it fulfils it. The intricate relationship of nature and grace, reason and revelation, was worked out superbly, and the resultant synthesis has not yet been abandoned by the Roman Catholic Church. But it was unable to forestall the savage attacks of Martin

Luther, who called the reason of unregenerate man a 'whore', and of John Calvin, who says, more politely, 'if men were taught only by nature, they would hold to nothing certain or solid or clear-cut, but would be so tied to confused principles as to worship an unknown god'.[15] The anti-rational tendency of orthodox Protestantism reached its climax in Karl Barth, who held implacably to the view that there is no point of contact between man and God, and slapped down the most distinguished of his followers, Emil Brunner, for trying to squeeze a little juice of truth from the dried orange of the human mind.[16] In between Luther and Barth Liberal Protestants had sturdily resuscitated the claims of natural theology, and some went so far as virtually to identify it with revealed theology, the latter being a somewhat more intense version of the former. ('Shakespeare was inspired but the Bible has a higher degree of inspiration'.)

But now we can draw attention to considerations which throw considerable doubt on all three traditional views, to a greater or less degree. There is no knowledge of God without revelation from God, and no knowledge of truth either, since all truth is God's truth. So far the liberals are right in holding that all knowledge is a form of revelation. But the deliverances of human reason, imagination and conscience are obscure and problematic, and the liberals are wrong in equating them with divine revelation as it is found, say, in the Bible. The Barthians are well-justified in saying that definitive knowledge of God is never attained by human enquiry, and is provided only by God himself, but wrong in denying all value to the human enquiry which moves towards the discovery of truth. The 'masterly compromise' of the

25

Schoolmen succeeds when it ascribes the findings of human reason to God's activity, but fails when it omits to take into account the confusions and contradictions of human reason and insight, which can by no stretching of the use of words be said to need only 'completion', but must at very many points be corrected or denied.

But if we say that human reason, prompted by the Spirit of God, puts the right questions, and suggests the available answers, and its contribution is thus entitled to be styled 'natural theology'; and that divine revelation is in a kind of dialogical relationship with this natural theology, sometimes confirming, sometimes denying its suggestions while answering its questions, then we have established the validity of human enquiry for Christian theology, and avoided both the natural opposition of revelation and reason and their equation with each other.

The relevance of all this to education, which has probably up to this point remained thoroughly obscure, is perhaps beginning to emerge. But before we draw this out in subsequent chapters, we must deal with a substantial objection that can be made to the line of thought so far pursued. This line of thought may have seemed to suggest, and could be held by its critics certainly to imply, that man takes or may take the initiative in the matter of the knowledge of God—whereas we know, both from the charter-document of the Christian religion, which is the Bible, and from the continuous development of Christian thought by both Catholic and Protestant theologians (more, some would say, by Protestants than by Catholics) that the initiative lies solely with God, not only in salvation but in illumination. To suggest otherwise smacks of the Pelagianism which must be avoided in the field of the intellect as much as in the field of will and action.

The objection rests on a confusion in theological thinking between the order of being *(ordo essendi)* and the order of knowing *(ordo cognoscendi)*. In the order of being God is absolutely prior to all things, to the entire universe; therefore he is the beginning of truth and knowledge, since all things take their origin from him. But in the order of knowing, man, with his desire to know, is prior, even to God; for without man there is no process of knowledge at all. Clearly the order of being is superior to the order of knowing, for it exists independently of the existence of the other order, and the reverse is not the case; so that man's initiative is secondary, and in no way infringes or denies the initiative of God. But it is a real initiative, and leads man towards truth, truth which is found ultimately alone in God. So God is both the starting point and the finishing point of all knowledge, and we can speak truly of the palindrome of revelation.

2

The Relevance of Theology

It may be that we have gone some way towards showing that in the Christian view of the universe not only does God reveal truth through the channels of revelation, such as the Bible and the Church, which have habitually been acknowledged as such by Christian tradition; he also enables, promotes and responds to human enquiry into truth—'he rewards those who search for him'.[17]

This theological statement now needs to be translated into the terms of the educational process as it is now understood. There is a kind of silent concordat between theologians and educationalists that they will operate in distinct universes of discourse, and need not, except in case of emergency, as when both religion and education are threatened by war or by an authoritarian government, engage in conversation together. This pact enables each party to formulate its theories and execute its practices without fear of being criticised or contradicted by the other. This fear is no doubt the more real because the areas of theology and education overlap so much. It is rather as if West and East Germany, with so many common interests, but afraid of each other's strength, had intentionally erected an Iron Curtain between themselves in order to be sure that each country had

28

complete freedom to do what it wanted to do without interference by the other.

Whether this be the motive or not, it is the fact that theologians, with certain honourable exceptions, such as the late Ian T. Ramsey[18], have paid little attention to education, except in the narrow sphere of religious education; and educationalists have tended to regard theology as an object of study far removed from their sphere of interest. This is under-standable in the case of educationalists who have set their faces against any claim of religion to truth; and in the case of theologians who, for pietistic or 'Barthian' reasons, restrict the area of theology to the direct commerce of the individual soul and of the Christian community with God. But it is not so easily excused in those who have a broader concept of education and theology, and many Christian educationalists and educationally-minded Christians are as prone to erect and maintain a barrier between these respective subjects as secularists and pietists. There are, no doubt, historical reasons for this—for instance, the long-overdue resolve of scientists, artists and philosophers to throw off the yoke of a prescribed theological system, and, in the end, of any theological system whatever, and the resentment caused in Churchmen by the loss of their valuable and long-held 'colonies'.

Whatever the reasons for the estrangement may be, the results are helpful to neither side. Theology loses the advantages of a stern critique from those whose business it is to formulate exact concepts of human development and to eliminate obscurity from the formulation of ideas which have to be communicated to the growing mind; and this is why it tends to depart into greater and greater isolation. Education misses the investigation of its values from the standpoint of historical Christianity, tends to express these values as if they stood on their own feet (which they cannot do), and builds a precarious empire on insecure foundations. We shall see the precariousness of this empire when we come to look at the views of Ivan Illich.[19]

Ian Ramsey has tried to destroy the barrier and to bring theologians and educationalists on to a common ground. He assumes that the purpose of education is to 'bring pupils to maturity', and he notes this maturity is for the most part seen in terms of Christian fulfilment (he is at this point speaking of boarding schools, but we may take it that his remark applies equally to the majority of other schools, whether or not they have an explicitly Christian basis). For him theology is 'the constant exploration of a disclosure-situation in terms of the models which those situations provide'. To those who are not versed in the terminology of Ramsey's philosophy of religion, this definition is no doubt obscure. Ramsey means by a 'disclosure-situation', a 'moment of vision' in which a man or woman becomes aware of that which transcends and gives meaning to the 'passing flux of immediate things' (this phrase comes from A. N. Whitehead). In older language, derived from Rudolf Otto, it is 'an experience of the numinous'. A 'model' is the image which we employ to make the experience which we have received articulate, and communicable (in a measure) to others. For instance (this is Ramsey's own example), a Hebrew shepherd who had received a vision of God's majesty would naturally express it in terms of the relationship between the shepherd and his sheep—hence the language of the twenty-third psalm and the prevalence of the shepherd-image in Biblical language, which is for the most part the language spoken by a partly-pastoral people.

Theology, then, according to Ramsey, is the exploration, the articulation of moments of vision in the terms available to those who have seen the vision, and derived from the situation in which they experienced it and from the culture to which they belong. The 'moment of vision', the 'disclosure-situation', of which Christian theology, in particular, is the exploration, is the recognition of the God of Abraham, Isaac and Jacob as incarnate in the words and life and death of Jesus Christ. Such theology is not uniform, monolithic, static—or it could not fulfil its task of doing justice to the variety of disclosure-situations in which Christians and others have found themselves, or to the inter-weaving of the many models, some transitory, some moderately permanent, which offer themselves; on the contrary, it is 'multiple' and 'variegated', and its 'very multiplicity and variegation point to an authority beyond themselves'.

It is within the framework of theology thus conceived that Christians ask that educational concepts such as obedience and command, authority and freedom, development and stimulation, should be considered, and it is out of this consideration that a Christian theology of education will emerge.[20]

Ramsey's approach to a theology of education might well be criticised as lacking all reference to the Godward aspect; he seems to place all his emphasis on the 'moments of vision' which human beings experience, and on the exploration of those moments in which they subsequently engage. But he surely holds that the visions are visions of *God,* and that the 'disclosure' in the 'disclosure-situation' comes from God; and these points are developed in his

31

other writings, in, for instance, his assertion of a theological interpretation of ethics 'which does not compromise the autonomy of ethics'.[21]

But he has vindicated the relevance of theology to education, and of education to theology, only in so far as the 'high moments' and fundamental issues of educational theory and practice are concerned. This vindication certainly demolishes a sizeable portion of the 'iron curtain' between the two disciplines. But education, as we all know, does not consist entirely of high moments and fundamental decisions; in fact, education in the classroom often entirely lacks these elements. In many a staff-room the posing of the question 'When did you last have a high moment or a fundamental issue in your class?' would provoke hollow and cynical laughter. Education for the most part is a humdrum business of arousing interest, maintaining order, assisting understanding, provoking curiosity, answering questions, giving information and indicating the sources of further information, and maintaining a corporate and co-operative spirit of enquiry.

These are at first sight purely technical matters, with no theological or philosophical or even ethical significance. They are the matters which the teacher is taught to handle in his College of Education, and his success in doing so depends entirely on his ability, temperament and training. The expertise is available, the books are accessible (and reasonably readable), the experience is attainable (either pleasurably or painfully), so why drag in 'highfalutin' considerations about the nature of reality or the relationship of God to man?

But this is seen to be a superficial attitude when it is remembered that the recipients of education as well as its dispensers, are people; for people, their characters and abilities, their strength and their weakness, their virtues and their faults, raise nearly all the philosophical and theological questions that anyone can think of. It is exceedingly foolish to say that Christian theology — or Muslim or Hindu theology for that matter — has nothing distinctive to say about them.

Here are some of the questions that call for an answer. Is a child in school being prepared for life on this earth only, or for eternal life? (This may be an embarrassing question, even for a Christian educationalist, but it is a basic and necessary one.) Has he within his own nature all the necessary abilities, even if they are inchoate or dormant, to grasp and retain the facts and their meaning which teachers wish him to have, or does he need 'spiritual' help, i.e. help from a divine source, to bring out and develop his powers to the full? Are such things as laziness and inattention, selfishness and cruelty, or, on the other hand, energy and concentration, helpfulness and sympathy, simply elements within him which result from his heredity, his environment and the structure of his own mind and emotions, and need to be discouraged or encouraged like propensities to eat harmful berries or nutritious proteins: or are they also open to ethical considerations and fitting objects of praise and blame?

Fascinating (though complex) books like *Language and Learning,* by James Britton,[22] tempt us to side-track these questions. Britton shows that language, which we all supposed was simply a means of communicating thoughts to another person, is also creative of the entire world of thought which makes up so much of our life. If this be so, and if we cannot

33

accurately indicate the origin of the language we use, except to say that the growing child uses and develops it naturally and unconsciously, what sense is there in asking basic questions about the meaning and purpose of life, or in uttering ethical judgements on the behaviour which results from doing what, quite literally, a child has told himself to do?

But the fundamental questions cannot be evaded so easily. Even if we accept Britton's theory up to the hilt, and agree that the values which we accept in later life are causally derived from the language which grew within us or was imposed by our teachers and our surroundings in infancy, we still have to ask whether language arises purely by chance, and has therefore no truth-relation, except coincidentally, with the world as it actually is, or in some other way; and whether the values are in any sense objective, or simply epiphenomenal (i.e. a spin-off from the human developmental process); and whether the child himself is at any point a free agent, able to choose his own destiny. Britton himself does not wholly evade these questions; he speaks at the end of his book of 'the need of the adolescent to be himself: to make important choices about himself and his work and his relationships; to match his individuation with involvement — intellectual, aesthetic, social, moral; to commit himself; to make independent decisions rather than merely keep promises; his need to be trusted'.[23] This seems to assert the objectivity of certain values, and the freedom of the individual to embrace them or not — and these are philosophical, if not theological, assertions; but the question-marks remain.

Other writers dodge the column by taking certain values for granted — values such as respect for persons and creative personal relationships, knowledge and understanding, individual autonomy, the disinterested desire for truth; and proceeding to characterise education (and educators) as good if it (and they) promotes these values in those being educated, and bad if it does not. Even writers so sophisticated and perceptive as P. H. Hirst and R. S. Peters in their *The Logic of Education*[24] are not entirely guiltless on this score. They do indeed submit 'values' and other educational concepts to rigid philosophical analysis, but they queer their own pitch by the adoption of a limiting definition of philosophy as being 'concerned with questions about the analysis of concepts and with questions about the grounds[25] of knowledge, belief, actions and activities'.[26] So we still have to ask: what if the values lauded by Hirst and Peters (remarkably similar to those approved by Christianity) are wholly repudiated by a subsequent generation or a different culture? Do they stand nevertheless? And what if the child to whom they are presented accepts them, and is entirely incapable of following them? 'Video meliora proboque, deteriora sequor'[27] is an exact description of a situation by no means limited to adults.

But the most popular evasion of the issue stems from a naively optimistic view of human nature, and of child nature. Such a view goes back, of course, to Rousseau. Some would trace it to Plato with his theory of *anamnesis,* according to which education is the process of bringing out into consciousness truths and values implanted in the mind during a previous incarnation. But no one who has read the *Republic* with care will think that Plato believed in the universal goodness of human nature. Rousseau, however, held that man is born good, a phrase

35

explained by G. D. H. Cole to mean that man's nature really makes him desire to be treated as one among others, and to share equally – man does *not* naturally want everything for himself, and nothing for others.[28] If this theory is applied to education, as it has been by Rousseau (in *Emile*) and his followers, it means that if the right intellectual, aesthetic and ethical values are put before children in a way which receives their attention and arouses their interest, they will respond by a developing love for them and come to live in a way which results from them. The best method is to take the child into the country, where he will become aware, by the help of a tutor (not his parents) of the ideas of obedience, duty and virtue, and make them his own. His interest in things around him is aroused, and leads to intellectual curiosity; and it is at this stage, and not before, that any kind of formal instruction is to be given. He should read *Robinson Crusoe,* in order to be led to imitate Crusoe in his discovery of his own needs and his ability to satisfy them. Foreign languages, history, religious instruction (of a neutral sort, leading him to decide for himself which faith he will adopt) and classical literature follow. (The words 'he' and 'his' are used, by the way, in the sexually limiting sense, since Rousseau was not so optimistic about girls, and expected them only to learn enough to make themselves pleasing to their husbands.)

All this was a lusty reaction from extravagant views in Catholic and Protestant circles, and current in society at large, of the depravity caused by original sin; and it promoted in many countries, for instance in Germany, where Moravian educationalists had been partial precursors of the same point of view, a desire to make education as widely available as possible. But why, in Rousseau's view, was previous education so unsuccessful and society so corrupt, if man was naturally good? His answer is, no doubt, in the *Social Contract,* where it is shown that man, naturally good, is preyed upon, oppressed and corrupted by external forces of greed and lust and ambition. But where else can greed and lust and ambition arise except in the heart of man? — which does not seem to be so naturally good after all. Besides, if we grant that man naturally approves and follows after the virtues of honesty, unselfishness, courage and love, what reason have we for being sure that other races and other cultures will not approve of other values? — as certain types of authoritarian society in our own time have certainly done. What meaning, at such a point, do we attach to the statement that man is naturally good?

In spite of these inconsistencies, Rousseau's views, in more and more sophisticated forms, have been maintained by many educational theorists ever since his time. Intense and exhaustive studies of the development of human cognition, intellection, volition and conation, and of the growing apprehension of ethical and aesthetic values, have proceeded on the assumption, and buttressed that assumption, that we have only to apply the right techniques of liberation from fear and anxiety and repression, and stimulate the nascent powers of learning and understanding that the child naturally possesses, and there will emerge from our schools a race of intelligent, altruistic, courageous, co-operative and transparently honest boys and girls such as the world has never seen before.

But the facts do not yet bear out this theory. It may be that the inadequate results of modern

education are due to the insidious effect of examina-
tions and other external pressures on the schools and
to the backlog of bad education in the past; and for
the rest to the human insufficiency of the teachers.
But these considerations, even if they are taken
together, do not really explain the unpleasant facts
of an age in which educational theory is more advanced and more widely known and practised than
ever before. It could be suggested that the traumatic
experience of many young teachers in their first posts
is due to the acceptance of a too-well-taught
College lesson that 'we needs must love the highest
when we see it'.

Pessimism is, however, another evasion of the
issue. It does not normally now take the form of
regarding human nature as irredeemable except by a
miraculous act of redemption performed by Christ on
behalf of the selected few. This was the old Calvinist
evangelicalism which had the doubtful merit of
assuring those who held it that they must be among
the righteous few, or they would not have been able
to see so plainly the plight of the wicked. Nowadays
it takes a deterministic, behaviouristic form (there is,
of course, a family resemblance between Calvinism
and behaviourism). We have now discovered, more
or less, how the minds and feelings of the young
operate; we know what happens when they learn, or
fail to learn, what is put before them: we have found
out what stimulates, or fails to stimulate, their
aggressive, altruistic and affective instincts and their
intellectual curiosity; we are aware of the real causes
and nature of the choices and decisions which they
make. All we have to do is to decide what the aims
of education are; to polish up our techniques and
communicate the way to use them to present and

future teachers; and then we can proceed to mould our pupils into being the acceptable citizens (acceptable to whom?) of the future (with the necessary statistical allowances for errors on the part of the educators and failures due to faulty mechanisms in the pupils).

This is the pessimism of depersonalization, akin to the state of mind which produces such ill-omened phrases as 'social engineering'. The attempt to encourage the growth of free persons in a free society is given up as hopeless, and we fall back on manipulating human beings in the most skilful way possible to be the kind of inwardly-propelled machines which fit most smoothly into the type of society that we consider best for them and for ourselves.

This low view of human nature is a philosophical possibility, and needs a great deal of philosophical investigation; it cannot, on any showing, be assumed to be true, as some writers tend to assume it. Its examination is part of the perennial debate between the advocates of free will and determinism which has gone on since man became a reflective individual. Here it can be said at once that the description of human nature which we have just given flies in the face of the moral judgement of humanity, and, if true, makes the words 'moral' and 'ethical' into meaningless noises. But we must also point out the inherent self-contradictions in the theory as a whole. Who is to decide what is the 'best' society for people to be fitted into? Not the Government, or the Church, or the people as a whole, but presumably the educators, themselves also presumably the impersonal mechanisms which they hold the rest of mankind to be.

If, then, there is a need after all for a philosophical

or theological adjudgement of man in the universe before we can be sure that we are erecting our system of education on a proper basis, and if many of the current bases of educational theory (often alleged, falsely, to be non-philosophical and non-theological) are, to say the least, debatable, it is open to a Christian theologian to offer a Christian theology of man and apply it to education. And it can be noted at the outset that such a theology, since it is a theology, not a scientific theory, does not at any point contradict any account of human development which can validate itself.

Man, according to orthodox Christian doctrine, is made in the image of God. This is both a misleading and a helpful statement, and it is in its helpful sense, of course, that we here commend it. If it is taken in the classical sense, which goes back to Irenaeus in the second century, it is misleading. According to this interpretation, man has inherent qualities of mind, spirit and will which are akin to those possessed by God, so that his mental and spiritual qualities put him at once in harmony with God, and he is able to understand the purposes of God. At least, this was the case before the Fall. At the Fall, alas, these qualities were disastrously damaged, so that man no longer — man in all the history which has followed the Fall — has the capacity to know and do the will of God. Some theologians have contended that he has lost this capacity altogether, and that all he does is absolutely sinful. Others have taken the milder view that his capacity is impaired at every point, but that he does succeed sometimes in doing what is good and thinking what is true.

In the strict tradition of Irenaeus himself and of official Roman Catholic theology, at least until

40

recently, this view is stated in a highly refined form. The distinction is made between 'the image' and 'the likeness' of God in man. The 'image' is made up of the 'ordinary' intellectual and moral qualities of man; the 'likeness' consists in the higher powers by which man knows and truly worships God. At the Fall man lost the likeness of God, and retained the image of God, so that he is still capable of truth and righteousness up to a certain limit. But Luther virtually demolished this double view by showing that it was based on a mistaken exegesis of Genesis 1,[27] where the words translated 'image' and 'likeness' in the older versions really mean exactly the same thing. So this view, if it is to be held at all, must be held in a form which does not distinguish the 'image' from the 'likeness' of God.

The difficulty about the classical view in any of its forms is not only that it easily runs away into the theory that God is made in the image of man, rather than the converse; but also that it makes out man to be a compound of qualities, and requires us to decide which of them are still effectively operating, and which are not. This is no way of dealing with man's nature and problems, as all modern psychology bears witness. It also raises awkward questions about the Fall of man as a historical event.

Luther points the way to a much sounder interpretation of the 'image of God', though he does not follow it very far himself. He shows us that the author of Genesis when he used the word 'image' was thinking in terms of personal relationship, figuratively described as the relationship between a mirror and the one who looks into it. God has made us in such a way that he expects to look at us and find a reflection of himself in us; and the ground of

41

his expectation is not that he has made us as replicas or dummies of himself (this is a very important part of the interpretation), but that his personal relationship with man creates in us those qualities through which we act and think as God acts and thinks.

Taken in this sense, the 'image of God' is a helpful concept. Whatever may be the defects of Luther's interpretation of Genesis (and it is plainly too complicated to have been in the mind of the author quite in the Lutheran form, and in any case the interpretation itself is not wholly coherent), it helps us to see that man is created as a *person* — though for much of his life, and through the whole of his youth, a person-in-process-of becoming — and a person not doomed to a solitary existence, 'poor, nasty, brutish and short', but from the start in a partly actual, partly potential relationship with God and his fellows. Man is never without God, whether he recognises this or not, for God does not cease in any circumstances to care for him; his relationship to God may be virtually one-sided (that is, it may be on God's side alone), it may be friendly, hostile or indifferent. But it is never absent. Man is never without his fellows: he may be literally or metaphorically autistic — at one extreme; or submerged in the mass of humanity — at the other; but the relationship does not disappear.

This, then, is the way to state the Christian view of man as he is created by God. What, then, of the Fall and its effects? So long as the word was understood in a historical sense, as, alas, many centuries of Christian tradition have insisted that it be understood, against the grain of liberal thinkers in every generation, there was no alternative to saying that man is depraved from birth (whether wholly or partly depraved does not matter very much), and thinking of children primarily as sinners needing to be redeemed, with alarming effects on the whole theory and practice of education wittily described by P. E. Sangster,[29] or rejecting the doctrine altogether and leaping across to the other extreme of unguarded optimism. But we are in this position no longer; it is now, surely, fairly clear that the doctrine of the Fall need not be, and should not be, interpreted as a view about history at all, any more than Hobbes' *Leviathan* or Rousseau's *Social Contract* are meant to be historical narratives. The doctrine of the Fall is about the nature of man wherever and whenever it is to be found. It does not describe the descent of man from the heights of moral perfection, or even of innocence, to the depths of corruption and depravity — like Lucifer falling from heaven. It intimates that man, the person-in-process-of becoming, and also the person-in-relation-to-God-and-other-persons, is in his very nature ambiguous. He aspires to the heights, he is drawn downwards to the depths — and this happens simultaneously, or in quick succession. He has great powers, and great weaknesses. He has the capacity for sustained and intricate thought, for prodigious feats of understanding and memory, and for the laborious application of his knowledge to the problems of his physical and mental life. He is capable of compassion and altruism and heroism and self-sacrifice, to the point of extreme patience and boundless endurance and ultimate self-sacrifice. He can also be lazy and muddled in his thinking, prejudiced and one-sided in his judgements. He can be utterly self-regarding, cruel, resentful and jealous. He can be carried away by the passions of greed, lust and ambition into actions of total irresponsibility and complete inconsiderateness for the feelings and interests of others. He frequently rises to lofty conceptions and noble plans, and fails at the last moment; but sometimes he carries them through to the highest fulfilment possible within the limitations of human existence. And when we say these things about 'man' in the general sense, we mean that in the wide-ranging variety of human personality and temperament, the capacities for good and evil of which we have spoken are always present in varying degree and strength.

It is odd that the first two chapters of Genesis, on which Christians have based the various doctrines of the Fall, should have been so frequently held to imply the absence of all good from post-lapsarian man. It may be that, in Britain at least, the influence of John Milton in *Paradise Lost* has been stronger than that of the plain meaning of Genesis. For Adam and Eve as they leave the Garden are not destitute of all virtues, or of all relationship with God; and their mutually opposite offspring, Cain and Abel, portray the double development of man as both evil and good.

In the light of this doctrine, the task of education, in simple terms, is to encourage the good in man and discourage the evil, and it is to these ends that a great deal of educational effort is in practice directed, whether the 'good' be understood intellectually, spiritually, emotionally, or morally. But this, though highly important, cannot be the sole task of education, though it may well seem to be quite big enough a task for any teacher or school. Man, in the Christian view, is man-in-relation, to God and his fellows; and 'fallen' man is in greater or less degree out of the proper relation to God and man, and sometimes wholly estranged. This breakdown in relationship,

44

whether it be complete estrangement, is what Christians call sin. In fact, it is the very essence of sin. And sin needs forgiveness, just as certainly as ignorance needs enlightenment. So education is incomplete without the Gospel of forgiveness, and the Gospel of forgiveness is incomplete without education; and both education and the Gospel are integral to the purpose of God for mankind.

But this last point needs expansion, and will receive it in the next chapter.

3

Education and Salvation

'Erasmus laid the egg which Luther hatched.' This has often been said in Reformation times and since. There is some truth in it. The writings of Erasmus, not least the satirical ones, his personal influence on rulers and scholars, and his immense prestige, all helped the other forces operative at the beginning of the sixteenth century to de-restrict philosophical and theological inquiry, to disperse the aura which surrounded the pronouncements and persons of notable ecclesiastics, to hold up monasticism to the light of critical investigation, and to call into question many teachings, ceremonies and practices which had gone unchallenged for centuries; and his Greek New Testament laid open to inspection and exegesis the authentically original words of Scripture. Without this last achievement, together with the invention of the modern style of printing, it is hard to see how Luther or any of the Reformers could have seen the new light which had broken forth from God's Word or communicated its new message to people at large. And all the other achievements of Erasmus conspired to create an atmosphere in which a Professor of Theology could question the tradition of the Church without being condemned out of hand by the world of scholarship, or dismissed as a blasphemous seducer by his own German *Volksgenossen.*

Moreover, Luther furthered Erasmus' ideal of restoring Christianity to its original simplicity in many respects, and borrowed several of his ideas. But in the relationship between the two men the most significant element was not their agreement but their disagreement, and this fact should discourage us from carrying too far the analogy of the laying and hatching of an egg. Presumably hens normally hatch eggs which are in large measure congenial to them — as the herring gull is willing to hatch the eggs of the black backed gull — but much of Erasmus' teaching and much of his attitude to Christianity and the Church was by no means congenial to Luther. Their differences came to a head in the debate about free will in 1521, when Erasmus disputed in his *De Libero Arbitrio* Luther's recent assertion that good works done with an eye to gaining the divine favour were damnable sins, maintaining that man is free to do good, though he does well to implore the help of God. Luther contested Erasmus' position in his violent and brilliant *De Servo Arbitrio,* ascribing man's salvation to God wholly and completely, denying the possibility of human co-operation, and accepting the doctrine of double predestination in all its harshness.[30]

The two men were arguing, and fundamentally disagreeing, about the nature of God and about human possibilities. Luther was ready to say that anything that God did, including the damnation of the wicked before they were born, was good, simply because God did it. Erasmus contended that God could not do anything that outraged justice. Luther held that human nature was powerless to do anything

47

A Christian Theology of Education

good; Erasmus held that human nature had numerous real potentialities for good of the highest sort.

The argument between the two men showed a crucial difference in thought between the representative of the Renaissance and the pioneer of the Reformation; for in the Renaissance man became vividly aware of human capacities, and was even prepared to limit the power of God, while the Reformation rejected any diminution of the divine prerogatives and discounted any statement about man which in the slightest degree called those prerogatives in question. The final severance of the two men was, historically, the parting of the ways for the Renaissance and the Reformation. And lest anyone should think that Luther's views at this time were untypical of his real thought, it should be remembered that Luther himself valued his book *De Servo Arbitrio* above all his other writings.

In the ensuing conflict the Reformation trampled on the Renaissance in its immediate effect on men's minds. In fact, it is scarcely an exaggeration to say that after the confrontation between Luther and Erasmus the Renaissance began to go underground. The ideas which had come to birth during the 'High Renaissance' period no longer influenced the academic and artistic world at large, and became the preserve of a few not very highly regarded people in Italy, Germany, France and England, while the Reformation in its various and divided forms seized the centre of the stage and was left to fight out alone the issue of Europe's religious future with the champions of the old religion, soon to be reinforced, united and made rigid by the Council of Trent. Insofar as the men of the Renaissance joined this continuing struggle, they were as likely to be found on the Catholic as on the Protestant side.

This cleavage between the Renaissance and the Reformation was disastrous in three respects at least. First, the humanistic, optimistic view of man and his capacities which we find in Leonardo and Erasmus and many of their contemporaries was soon declared to be in stark opposition to the Christian view of man as a fallen creature, whether in its Catholic or its Protestant form. There is, of course, a tension between Renaissance and orthodox Christian approaches to human nature. But in the thought of the more serious Renaissance thinkers, for instance, Erasmus and Leonardo themselves, and, in this country, Colet and Thomas More, there was no disposition to make man out to be omnicompetent and wholly autonomous. Man was, no doubt, a superb creature, and lord of creation, and called to take part in the work of creation. But he was still under God, still liable to temptation, still needing redemption and enlightenment from God. And even the pessimistic Protestant view of man as propounded by Luther and Calvin, formed no doubt partly under Renaissance influence (which they personally would have repudiated), allowed that human reason, though fallen with the rest of human nature, could grasp the principles of logic and law and the natural sciences, and could even bring order into political life by controlling violence in the name of God and making just laws to regulate social relationships.

But when the two parties were driven into downright opposition to each other, each pushed its views to logical extremes. Man's achievements were exaggerated and his failures minimised in the humanism which flourished in certain quarters. Still more,

49

in the other camp, man's utter sinfulness and total depravity were stressed to the point of (as we should think) blasphemy against the God who was alleged to have created beings guilty of such foulness and outrage. Both of these tendencies became obvious in the eighteenth century, when the Renaissance, now re-named the Enlightenment, or the Age of Reason, came out of hiding and published its views far and wide, and evangelical Christianity polished up and promulgated its notion of the 'plan of salvation'; but they were inherent in a great deal of the thinking that preceded these outbursts.

This bitter conflict that should never have happened is perhaps best seen in an unexpected place, Shakespearean tragedy. For there, and most notably in *Hamlet,* the two developments are captured by the vision of the poet just before their final dissociation from each other, and their interplay constitutes a major element in the spiritual dilemma of the tragic hero. Hamlet's apostrophe to man seems to epitomize the Renaissance view of him:

'What a piece of work is a man! How noble in reason! how infinite in faculty! in form, in moving, how express and admirable! in action, how like an angel! in apprehension how like a god! the beauty of the world! the paragon of animals.'[31]

Here we have the glorification of reason and the ascription to man of angelic, nay, god-like, qualities. And this is the concept of man which comes to Hamlet from his education and some of his own inclinations; it is the concept of man to which he strives to be true, and to which he expects his friends to be true, so that he praises Horatio for his freedom from passion. But the apostrophe to man ends in disillusionment, and its mood throughout is questioning, rather than asseverative:

'And yet to me, what is this quintessence of dust? Man delights not me; no, nor woman either ...'

And in other moods he can give expression to a view of man not very far removed from that of Augustine as interpreted by Luther.

'I am very proud, revengeful, ambitious: with more offences at my beck than I have thoughts to put them in, imagination to give them shape, or time to act them in. What should such fellows as I do, crawling between heaven and earth? We are arrant knaves, all; believe none of us. Go thy ways to a nunnery!'[32]

Perhaps Hamlet here exaggerates his sentiments, but so he does in the opposite direction when he apostrophizes man in his glory. And as to his friend, that man of reason, we know that Hamlet thought that there were more things in heaven and earth than were contemplated in Horatio's philosophy. (There is an excellent discussion of this issue in Ivor Morris: *Shakespeare's God*)[33]

Caught between these two views of man which he cannot reconcile, Hamlet involves himself in his inescapable doom. Perhaps they are in principle irreconcilable anyway, and in their extreme form they certainly are. But they could have lived together in a truly reformed Christianity, and Christian humanism could have remained a live option for many, whereas in fact it was so only for those choice and select spirits, the Christian Platonists, and a few others.

The second calamitous effect of all that was implied by the Luther-Erasmus breakdown was the divorce between education and religion. It did not show itself at once. The Reformers in each country knew well that education could be the primary agency for the dissemination of their ideas and for changing the pattern of Christian worship and theology. They were also greatly concerned, as pastors, for the spiritual welfare of the young, who could become again, as they had been in the past, easy victims of what they believed to be superstition and heresy; so that, above all, they must be made deeply acquainted with the true message of the Bible. Therefore with the Reformation went the tireless building-up of schools and other places of learning. For their part, the promoters of the Catholic Reformation (which is the better way of indicating what has usually been called the Counter Reformation) saw just as clearly the need for education in the principles of the Tridentine faith, and in the Society of Jesus they had to hand an instrument which for their purposes could scarcely be bettered; Jesuit educational institutions sprang up not only in Europe but in all the areas of Catholic missionary enterprise.

But Protestant and Catholic schools, from the modern point of view, both had a built-in flaw. However good they were in method and syllabus and in the quality of teaching, they were 'closed' schools, existing for the ultimate purpose of promulgating a particular theological system. This was entirely justifiable from their point of view; it was, after all, the aim of their founders, and of their supporting churches. And if there had not been schools of this sort, there would have been virtually no schools at all. The ecclesiastical authorities in each case were convinced in their hearts and marrows that the truths of Christianity as they saw them were 'saving' truths, without the knowledge of which men and women might well be condemned to perdition.

The practical moral of this was obvious. This is not the stage at which to argue the rights and wrongs of this position, though its supporters need to put up a very strong case if they are to justify the continued existence of their schools (and this they are not unwilling to do). The precise point at the moment is that when humanism in the form of rationalism and empiricist philosophy, now reinforced and encouraged by the rapid advance in scientific knowledge which was just beginning, emerged into the open at the end of the seventeenth century, it proceeded to declare war on the confessional schools, as the homes of obscurantism and the enemies of free enquiry. The Religious Academies set up by Nonconformists in England gave little support to this charge, and we all know that a good school, if the teachers are of the right sort, can unobtrusively overcome the difficulties created by its fundamental principles. But in the eyes of the humanists these were mere palliatives of an objectionable system — just as the merits of many independent schools are regarded by socialists who wish to abolish them altogether. And it is, of course, true that even in such otherwise enlightened institutions as John Wesley's Kingswood, which included science in its curriculum considerably in advance of its contemporaries,[34] small children and those not so small were emotionally dragooned into the experiences of guilt and conversion which were required by the exigencies of evangelical theology; while other confessional schools which lacked the religious excitement of Kingswood did not have its enlightenment either.

It was easy enough, therefore, to argue that education conducted by Christian teachers was liable to infringe the principles laid down in John

Locke's *Letters on Toleration.* 'We should do well to commiserate our mutual ignorance, and endeavour to remove it in all the gentle and fair ways of information: and not instantly treat others ill, as obstinate and perverse, because they will not renounce their own and receive our opinions.'[35] But whether it was explicitly argued or not, the opposition remained. The triumph of one party in France at the time of the Revolution led, as was to be expected, to the complete secularization of French schools. In a milder fashion, religion was ceremoniously expelled from all schools by the Founding Fathers of the American Republic. Only in Britain, of the countries where the Church has been dislodged from the seat of power, do Church schools enjoy the support of the State, and this is widely regarded as an anomaly even by those who do not dare to remove it. Even here, under the calm surface of the Dual System, in the staff rooms of state schools in which religious education is legally compulsory, and of public schools on an ecclesiastical foundation where religious education is taken for granted (and not often carried out very effectively), there is a persistent tension between those who think that their task is education, and the smaller number of those who conceive it in terms of evangelism; because of the evil history which goes back to the time of Erasmus and Luther, it does not seem to occur to either side that education and religion are not necessarily in opposition or competition, and that enlightenment and evangelism may possibly belong together.

But the most serious consequence of all was the failure to retrieve the Bible's teaching about the purpose of God for man at the very time when the Bible lay open for fresh inspection. Erasmus, for all his Biblical scholarship, reduced Christianity to enlightened Platonic common sense and good morals, based on the imitation of Christ, in his *Enchiridion Militis Christiani*. (The title is probably a pun. It could mean either a 'little sword' or a 'handbook' for the Christian soldier.)[36] Thus he fell foul both of Catholics and of Protestants. To Catholics he seemed to have repudiated the sacramental system by means of which alone a man may receive salvation on earth and felicity in heaven. Erasmus' semi-detached attitude to the sacraments may have appealed to Protestants on the left wing, but by no means endeared him to Luther, while his complete failure, in Luther's eyes, to understand the desperation of the human predicament caused by sin, and the magnificence of God's grace given to sinners through justification by faith alone, persuaded the Reformers that Erasmus was not very far from being an enemy of the Gospel.

So here again entrenched positions were gradually taken up. The humanists, whether they called themselves Christians or not, maintained that man was brought to maturity and true happiness by the illumination of his mind (for reason is the 'candle of the Lord') and virtuous behaviour. The Catholics taught that the stain of original sin was wiped out by baptism alone and that man was nourished in the way of blessedness by participation in the Mass, and could not be nourished without it. The Churches of the Reformation — even the sober Church of England, in spite of its natural propensity to Erasmianism — proclaimed that sinful man could be rescued from his extremity and the imminence of damnation only by faith in the redemptive work of Christ carried out on the Cross.

So three different views of salvation — intellectual-moral, sacramental-priestly, and solifidian (i.e. that faith without works is sufficient for salvation) propagated themselves in separation from each other and in conflict with each other. The intellectual-moral view could find support in Scripture — are not the prophets and the Gospels full of moral teaching? does not Jesus appeal to human reason with his statements about God's love? — but it did little justice to the strength of human passions and the intermittent weakness of the human will. It goes without saying that Catholics and Protestants each held that their view was the only one that Scripture and authentic Christian tradition supported.

Here is revealed, not simply a dispute between discrepant views of God's providence and man's nature, not simply a conflict between education and evangelism, but a carving into three of the Biblical doctrine of salvation itself. The Bible recommends the constant appeal to human reason and conscience, as in: 'Come now, let us argue it out, says the Lord'; and Paul's 'we recommend ourselves to the common conscience of our fellow-men'.[37] The Bible is rich in sacramental practices and instructions to make use of them. The Bible lays immense stress on the free grace of God and the indispensability of faith. But what has happened all too frequently in Christian history, especially since the Reformation, is that men of reason have discounted faith and the sacraments, the sacramentalists have undervalued faith and reason, and evangelists have rejected reason and the sacraments.

Now when this is done by any one of the three schools of thought, it can make its position intellectually respectable only by accepting the partition of human personality which comes down to us in various versions from Plato, but in all its forms implies the absolute distinctness of body and soul, and usually involves the absolute distinctness of body, *mind* and soul. Once this partition is made — and it is not too much to say that it is as venerable a part of Catholic and much Protestant orthodoxy as the doctrine of the Trinity itself — it seems obvious to all concerned that education is a matter of the mind and body (chiefly the mind, except in some public schools), and religion is a matter of the soul. The high-theological statement of this is that there are two kingdoms under God: the kingdom of this world, where the Devil may be supposed to exercise his regency, and the kingdom of God. The one kingdom comprises man's physical, mental, social, economic and political activities. The other relates solely to his spiritual life in the community of the faithful, in prayer and worship and Christian fellowship. It is obvious that this doctrine of the two kingdoms can take either a Catholic or a Protestant form. In simple terms it means that Jesus came to save men's souls, that souls are immortal, that the cultivation of the soul is the highest human exercise, and that heaven is inhabited by the souls of the righteous. The bodily and mental needs of man, in comparison with the needs of his soul, are unimportant. They are not, indeed, to be neglected (for the parable of the Good Samaritan has never been entirely forgotten); but their satisfaction is a work of charity, enjoined on Christians as the consequence of their faith and an exercise of their love; but the faith and love themselves are the turning of the soul towards God, and only afterwards, and not even necessarily (though, of course, acceptably to God) the turning of man towards his neighbour. And responsibility for society, for politics and economics, for reform and the liberation of the oppressed are seen as *applications* of the Gospel, not as integral parts of the Gospel; and they can be dispensed with, to no spiritual loss, by those whose interests and needs are solely concerned with their own inner life.

This error has bitten deep into the consciousness of Christendom: so much so that in most Christian circles still today a Christian who busies himself in social or political matters, aside from the exercise of straightforward charity, is thought of as somehow 'unspiritual'; anyone who casts doubt on the proposition that each of us has an immortal soul is thought to have denied the Christian doctrine of the life to come; it is still seriously argued whether a Christian ought to take part in politics, though politics is primarily the organisation of human life in society. Strangest of all, some of the most powerful defenders of the Christian faith in our time are committed to the complete separation of the sphere of the soul from the sphere of the body and to the vilification of the body, in Manichaean fashion, and see nothing but evil in the attempt of the World Council of Churches to influence national and international policies. Others have resuscitated (perhaps without realising it) the doctrine of Luther about the Two Kingdoms in its starkest form, so that the treatment of immigrants and the politics of power and wealth are alleged to have nothing whatever to do with the Gospel. Luther and Erasmus, and the battalions ranged behind them, have much to answer for!

But the end of this long period of obfuscation and vain dispute is now perhaps in sight, for the good reason that what the Bible says about salvation is being uncovered by critical scholarship. This has happened as a result, mainly, of two developments. The primary one is the liberation of Biblical studies from dogmatic trammels and the employment of scientific, 'humanistic' methods for the elucidation of scripture. This development is now of long standing, and its completion is hindered only by the persistence of Conservative Evangelical theology, which still tends, though now with modified strictness, to dictate to the Biblical student in advance what his conclusions are to be. It needs no further comment here. Secondary, but very important, is the liberation of theology from denominational trammels. This is one solid result of the Ecumenical Movement, and is now proceeding apace, though it has still a long way to go. 'Ecumenical theology', like any other process of human thought, has passed through many phases, though its history is so short. It has been strongly influenced in turn by Protestant liberalism, Anglo-Catholic ecclesiolatry, Barthian Biblicism with a strong whiff of eschatology, and secular radicalism. The theology of the Orthodox Churches was late in adding its contribution, and Roman Catholic theology was later still. But the eventual confluence of all these streams of thought has led to a balance hard to gain, and harder to retain, but certainly present now in embryo. For many years great efforts were needed to reconcile within the Faith and Order Movement the claims of Protestant and Catholic conceptions of grace, faith and the sacraments, and of Protestant and Catholic views of the Church and the ministry; and the new ecumenical understanding of Biblical concepts was an indispensable aid in this struggle.

But at the Fourth Assembly of the World Council

A Christian Theology of Education

of Churches in Uppsala in 1968 a new dimension was added to the ecumenical conversation — the issues of liberation from oppression and the needs of the Third World. Of course, the World Council of Churches had always, from its inception, proclaimed itself to be in favour of freedom and justice, and had taken practical steps, in the shape of Christian Aid, to bring material help to refugees and the myriad other needy people of the world. This had always been thought to be a proper outworking of Christian love, now made possible on a grand scale by the coming-together of the Churches. But it had not been thought to be a *theological* issue — it was simple charity. But at Uppsala the Third World forced its entrance into the theological scene, asking insistently: what is the theological condemnation of racism? what is the theological justification of liberation movements? what is the theological significance of world development and aid to new countries? of the secularization of Western Society? of the demand for universal education? Are these matters peripheral to the Christian world view — optional adjuncts, for those who are interested in such things or find it convenient to promote them for their own purposes — or are they central to the Christian message?

These new questions created new uproars, especially among those Christians who had been already left behind by the advance of ecumenical thinking; and the uproars were focussed in the discussion of the World Council of Churches' Special Fund for financial aid towards the social and educational activities of certain liberation movements. The serious disputants went back to their Bibles, and looked there for the relation between salvation, liberation and education; and the administrators planned and carried out the Conference at Bangkok in 1972 which had the title 'Salvation Today'.

What then is the Biblical doctrine of salvation? It is far from simple, and any statement about it is limited by the presence of more than one strand of thought in the New Testament itself. But it can be said at the outset that it is not by any means restricted to the 'way to heaven' of the individual, as even John Wesley thought it was.

It starts with the Hebrew view of the human personality (long understood by scholars, but till recently reserved to them) which runs right through the Old and New Testaments, developing in the process. Man — each man and woman — is a living being,[38] a psycho-physical totality; and the word which expresses this in Hebrew is inadequately and misleadingly translated 'soul' in most versions. This living being contains three elements — the material substance which is called 'flesh', the basis of all activity, created by God for good purposes; the 'spirit', which is the seat of thought and the point of contact between God and man; and the 'heart', which is the seat of will and the control of thoughts and feelings. But these three elements are in no sense separated, and the functions of one run easily into those of another; still less is there any partition, or any trace of the idea that they have any independent existence, or rights of their own. They exist for the purpose of fulfilling their function within the wholeness of the one living being, the soul. Man has no soul; he *is* a soul, but a soul in the sense just defined.

These ideas appear in a slightly changed form in the New Testament. Here it is the word 'body' which defines man as a unitary, living being; it is the nearest

61

equivalent anywhere in the Bible to our word 'personality'; it indicates the unity in which all the organs
and members comprise a harmonious and cooperative
whole. 'There are many different organs but one
body.'[39] There is no human existence which is not
'bodily', and the resurrection of the body is the
resurrection of the total self.

But man, as one whole, can also be called 'soul'.
He *has* no soul; he *is* a body, he *is* a soul. The 'soul'
is the same entity as the 'body', looked at as the
personal life of an individual being with consciousness,
will and activity. But man is also 'flesh' — with reference to the material substance which enables him to
eat and drink and move. When the New Testament
describes man as 'flesh', or as 'flesh and blood', it is
simply referring to his existence as a material being;
for other points of view, as we have seen, he is called
'body' and 'soul'. But sometimes the New Testament,
recognising that the physical part of human nature
is the seat of appetites and passions, extends the
neutral meaning of 'flesh' to signify the sensual,
self-asserting drives of human nature which have the
character of sin.[40]

Thus the emphasis all the way through is on the
oneness of human beings, their 'personalities', their
existence which is at once physical, mental and
emotional. And from this it follows at once that many
of the most familiar and 'orthodox' notions of man
in Christian thought are unbiblical. There are, in the
Biblical account, no such entities at all as souls
without bodies, or souls inhabiting bodies; it is not
so much the case that the doctrine of the immortality
of the soul is untrue, as that it is Biblically incon-
ceivable. The resurrection of the body is, then, not a
doctrine of natural immortality, as some have

interpreted it; nor of the re-assembly of our physical elements at the Day of Judgement, as others have thought. It is a doctrine asserting the grace of God who gives eternal life to us though we are physically dead — to us as 'bodies', total unitary personalities, expressing ourselves and communicating with others by such means as may be appropriate to life in heaven. And there is no ground for holding that the Bible condemns our physical nature or regards it as anything but God's creation.

It goes without saying that the many misunderstandings to which we have referred are not solely due to human perversity or dogmatism. Many of them arise from the familiar usage of the words 'soul' and 'body' in English and other modern languages; in ordinary speech, under distant Greek influence, they have meanings, and carry implications, which are quite contrary to Biblical teaching. Unless this is grasped, it is very difficult indeed for anyone to go on to understand the Biblical doctrine of salvation.

The words 'save', 'salvation' and 'saviour' pass through many stages of meaning in the Biblical period, but the development is continuous and harmonious. The sense first encountered is never lost; and it is simple and direct. To be 'saved' is to be rescued from disaster — defeat, captivity or death, or all three. This is salvation in a plainly material and concrete sense. The terms are much more often used corporately than individually in the Old Testament; many passages in the Psalms which speak in the first person singular give a different impression, but the 'I' in the Psalms is to be taken as liturgical very often, and perhaps nearly always; the individual psalmist is speaking for the nation. And when 'salvation' occurs it is the work of God; God is the Saviour, the liberator of his people.

In later parts of the Old Testament salvation sometimes refers specifically to deliverance from sin and to the inward joy which results from this. But this is quite uncommon, and does not exclude the material, 'political' sense of the word. More often the concept is generalized beyond the nation and related to God's entrance into the historical process as the ruler of all mankind; and here also the purpose of his entrance is the freedom of his people and the inauguration of peace and righteousness and love throughout the whole creation.

When Jesus comes on the scene as Saviour, it cannot be too strongly emphasized that his saving work, though it is necessarily limited during his earthly career to the welfare of individuals and families and small groups of people, is all-inclusive in its scope. He performs direct acts of deliverance for people in physical need; he forgives sins; he sets free those who have been taken captive; and, before he sets out to do all this, he announces his programme in the synagogue at Nazareth:

> The spirit of the Lord is upon me because
> he has anointed me;
> he has sent me to announce good news to
> the poor,
> to proclaim release for prisoners and recovery
> of sight for the blind;
> to let the broken victims go free,
> to proclaim the year of the Lord's favour.[41]

Of course, the announcement of God's forgiveness which we so frequently find on the lips of Jesus is an integral part of this, but it is not the case that while forgiveness is essential, the other activities of Jesus are ancillary. Forgiveness and all his other activities belong together as one whole, which is Jesus' work for the salvation of mankind.

Jesus' saving activity in Palestine was bound to be for individuals, as we have seen, and bound to be mostly limited to Jews. But after the Ascension his farthest-seeing friends rightly understood that all the limitations were now removed; in fact, it is no doubt their understanding of this that underlies the narrative of the Ascension itself. What Jesus did was to inaugurate God's kingdom, to give a foretaste, an earnest, a starting-point of the salvation which God intended for the whole created order in every part. That salvation began with Jesus; it was continued in the Church; it was meant for all men and it covered the whole of human life; it was to be finally consummated (sooner or later, and Jesus' disciples probably thought it would be sooner) by God's final winding-up of all human affairs. So Paul truly interpreted the message of his Lord when he wrote:

'The created universe waits with eager expectation for God's sons to be revealed. It was made the victim of frustration, yet always there was hope, because the universe itself is to be freed from the shackles of mortality and enter upon the liberty and splendour of the children of God'.[42]

It is therefore man as soul (not the soul of man), as body, as a person, as a whole, that is to be saved, that is already being saved; man corporate, and not only man individual; man physical, mental and spiritual, and not only man spiritual; man in his personal life, man in his social, political and economic life; man in relation to man as well as to God, man under pressure from inward drives, his own past and the history and present of his people and nation

65

and race; man in his sexual, intellectual, emotional life; man who is incomplete and immature until all his society is mature and complete. It is for man in his total nature that Jesus died, rose and ascended; and even man is not the boundary of God's salvation, for its scope includes the whole created order.

But Christian teachers have habitually spiritualized, internalized and individualized all this, allegorizing or denying the plain meaning of Biblical language. Not that the individual and his inner spiritual needs are outside God's salvation. On the contrary, there is a very important sense in which the forgiveness of a man's sins, the establishment of his peace with God, his growth in love and holiness, his prayers and his individual participation in worship and Christian fellowship, have priority over all the other elements in God's purpose for him, for only insofar as he has accepted these blessings is he free to be an uninhibited, responsible, creative agent in the furthering of God's saving purpose for the world. But it is a serious and disaster-laden error to suppose that God's saving activity stops at the individual, or at the Church. Each man needs to be saved from his sins, and God has provided the way for this to happen. The Church must proclaim forgiveness, and communion with God and sanctification, and embody these in its corporate life and in the life of its members, and make them available to all men by its preaching and its sacraments. But God's salvation goes on and on, and out and out; its only frontiers are the frontiers of the universe itself.

Salvation, then, on the Biblical understanding of it, includes the forgiveness of sins; it includes the liberation of mankind; it includes education. Liberation and education are not ancillaries to

religion and the Gospel; they are not outworkings
or applications of the Gospel. They are integral
parts of the Gospel. We do not need to look for the
ethical, social, political or educational *implications*
of the Gospel; we need to search *within the Gospel
itself* for what God is doing and wishes us to do in the
fields of political and economic action and in education.

The relation, then, of education to salvation is
that of the part to the whole; and if it be, as it is,
God's purpose for mankind that each member
of it, both as himself and in community, should
become wholly mature vis à vis God, himself and
other people, then education has a vital role in the
fulfilment of God's purpose, a role which both
theologians and educationalists neglect at their
peril, and all Christian teachers to their infinite
shame.*

* A very similar account of the Biblical concept of Salvation is
powerfully expounded by Pauline Webb in her *Salvation Today*.[43]

4

Christian Motives

The achievements of the Christian Church in the field of education are undeniably impressive. As the Roman Empire was gradually Christianized, and Christian teachers of the young took over from their predecessors — rudely called 'pagan', more properly styled 'Hellenistic' — they did not in most cases repudiate the educational traditions of the past. Sometimes they thought that they were doing so —'what has Athens to do with Jerusalem, the Academy with the Church?' asked Tertullian — and intended to do so; but without a self-conscious return to barbarism, which was the last thing they had in mind, it was impossible to cast off the categories and the methods which were in fact the only ones available. So when Jerome, reproved in a dream of judgement on what he thought was his deathbed for being Ciceronian rather than Christian, proceeded to try to become more Christian in his approach to intellectual matters, nothing fundamental happened to his modes of thinking, although thereafter he paid more attention to the Hebrew and Greek Scriptures than to his much-loved classical authors.[44]

But to the Greek notion of 'paideia', suffused already with Roman ideas of order and discipline, Christian teachers added the content of the Christian

Gospel and its concern with the illiterate 'barbarian' as well as with the Graeco-Roman intellectual élite. Through the long centuries of political confusion and intellectual marking-time which we call the Dark Ages, the monasteries still practised the education of their members and of others outside their walls; and when Charlemagne decided to educate the 'barbarians' whom he had subdued, he called in Alcuin of York to set up a model school at Tours, and to furnish it with a comprehensive library. Alcuin himself wrote educational manuals, and promoted the dialogue method of instruction. The activities which he encouraged mark the real starting-point of the movement which produced the lecture-rooms of the Schoolmen and the Universities of the Middle Ages.

The Reformation gave a powerful fillip and a new direction to educational enterprise, and until the nineteenth century was well on its way it was mostly at the instigation of Churchmen in both Protestant and Roman Catholic countries that kings and other national rulers, or in other cases rich merchants and municipalities, set up schools and maintained them. Nor is it easy to see how universal education would have been initiated in this country, and others, if the Christian impulse had not been present. The disgraceful rivalries of the denominations in England during the nineteenth century obscure but do not entirely discredit the contribution of the Churches to the education of the industrialized masses.

In due course the quarrels of the Churches and their lack of financial resources made it urgently necessary for the State to take over most of the work of education, and it is at least arguable that it would have been better if the takeover had been complete from the start. But the original contribution of the Churches remains, and its effect for good is not yet entirely spent. Those who have received education and educational institutions from the Churches have usually shown themselves no more grateful than the one-time British colonies, now independent, have shown themselves grateful for British rule. But gratitude is rare in human affairs, and in any case the secular authorities can in this instance justifiably complain that the legacy which they received contained evil as well as good.

The same pattern of Christian pioneering and secular development is to be found overseas within the area of the British Commonwealth. Few schools and colleges were founded there in the early days by anyone except missionaries, and 'missionary' schools and colleges are still essential in many areas, if education, lower or higher, is to be continued at all. But the changeover is already in full swing, and it is a difficult issue of missionary policy whether the schools and colleges in question should be held on to and fought for, or gladly surrendered to the national authorities.

The achievement, then, is immense. But when we inquire into the motives behind this long-standing and continued educational activity by the Christian Churches, we enter an area of great uncertainty. It should be said first of all that all human enterprises, however splendid in intention or result, or both, spring from mixed motives, and the Christian educational enterprise is no exception. Second, it should be said that the ascription of motives by historians to men and women long dead is a very precarious matter, even when, and sometimes especially when, the people concerned have published

their motives in open documents (or their septu-
agenarian memoirs). The imputation of low motives
to persons thought widely to be honourable is a
common and serious failing of certain economic and
psychological historians; and it is the more difficult
to counteract because the authors in question can
reply to any contrary evidence by arguing that the
alleged motives are unconscious.

This said, some tentative suggestions can be made
about Christian motives in the history of education.
In the early centuries, when Christianity was still
fighting for its life, or making small and arduous
steps forward, the main motives of Christian teaching
were the instruction of converts and the children of
believers in the faith, and the persuasion of 'pagans'
that Christian belief was intellectually sound. These
motives were certainly prominent in the Catechetical
School of Alexandria (which was not such a formal
institution as its usual name implies), where Clement
and Origen emerged as masterly apologists; general
education was, no doubt, ancillary.

During the Dark Ages the Church was responsible
for all the education there was. This was, outside the
monasteries, not very much, but the teachers had
to be wide in their scope. The motive was certainly
not least evangelistic, and in some areas it was
directly designed to promote the orthodox, catholic
faith against the Arian heresy which had spread far
and wide over the Germanic countries. Later it came
to be more and more assumed that everyone was a
Christian in religion, and the educational principles
of the Middle Ages were formulated on that assumption; the purpose of medieval Universities was not to
argue *about* the truth of Christianity, but to argue
within the truth of Christianity as to its understanding

71

and articulation, and its relation to all human intellectual pursuits. This is why theology was the Queen of the Sciences; her priority was not a sacerdotal imposition, but the necessary consequence of the medieval world-view. The 'quadrivium' of music, arithmetic, geometry and astronomy, and the 'trivium' of grammar, rhetoric and dialectic, were in the last resort means to the end of theology.

Yet it would be absurd to conclude that in the Dark Ages or (even more absurd) in the Middle Ages there were no teachers who valued knowledge for its own sake or students who pursued the sciences without an ulterior theological motive.

In the Reformation period and afterwards, as we have already seen, the prime purpose in the setting up of schools, directly or indirectly, by the Churches, was the promulgation of the catholic or the reformed, or, in England, the Anglican, faith. Yet other considerations were also prominent. When John Colet founded St. Paul's School in 1509 and provided for 'a hundred and fifty and three (scholars) to be taught free in the same, in good literature, both Latin and Greek', he laid it down in his Statutes that the masters should instruct the children by reading to them 'such authors that hath to wisdom joined the pure chaste eloquence'. The authors listed in the first curriculum of the school, drawn up with the help of Erasmus, include many Latin authors, but none from the classical period; but there is good reason for thinking that Terence and Cicero and Virgil soon found their way into the classroom. Colet himself had some moral objections to many classical authors, and other faults, he thought, had corrupted the pure Latin of Cicero and Sallust; he therefore laid great stress on the teaching of grammar and of a pure style of writing. He also instituted the study of Greek with the same emphases. He thus added linguistic and literary training, the sixteenth century equivalent of several subjects on the modern time-table, to instruction in the unadulterated Gospel of Jesus Christ and the ethical principles to be derived from it.[45]

In another country and at a later period, Johannes Amos Comenius and his disciples travelled far beyond the confines of confessional indoctrination in the kind of schools which they advocated. Comenius was a bishop among the Bohemian Brethren (or the Moravians, as we now call them), and he held that education was the most effective means of establishing that spiritual unity of all Christians for which he prayed and struggled. The immediate purpose of schools was to train the pupils in the 'pansophia', the harmony of all aspects of the divine wisdom. This was to be done by persuasion, not coercion, and by the full use of the senses; the mere accumulation of knowledge was to be discouraged, and nothing was to be learned which had not previously been understood. Above all, the schools were to be informed and inspired by the 'Unum Necessarium', which is love.[46] The influence of Comenius, outside and inside his own communion, is agreed to have been considerable.

We have spoken already of the Dissenting Academies in seventeenth and eighteenth century England with their comprehensive syllabuses, and of the encouragement of science in John Wesley's Kingswood.[47] The educational history of England in the nineteenth century is dominated by the attempt of partisan groups to gain the children for their own confessional purposes, and by the emergence

73

in Thomas Arnold's Rugby and its many imitators of the ideal of the English gentleman in the Anglican mould. Very often in nineteenth century schools (though not at Rugby) the impulse of denominational chauvinism is naked and unashamed. But we dare not discount the quite different motivation of many who served — and governed — under an uncongenial system and succeeded somehow in preserving their educational integrity. The tensions thus created ran right through the Colleges of Oxford and Cambridge, and the church-sponsored Teachers' Training Colleges; they constituted an important factor in the complicated process which led to the foundation of the University of London.

It is surely clear that in the history of Christian schools and colleges we have a welter of motives at work from almost the highest to almost the lowest. And some of them which seem to us in our time to be dubiously creditable, such as the replacement of a pagan-barbarian culture by a Christian one, were not in their historical context questionable or questioned. But the insertion of the word 'almost' before 'the highest' hints that there may be a more excellent way now open to us (perhaps open in the past, perhaps not), than any of those so far marked out. And the discrediting of dogmatic and denominational motivation by Christians and non-Christians alike suggests that the time has come for inquiring whether such a way exists.

God, we venture to repeat, is the fountain of revelation about himself and the universe. With his revelation about the universe we are not at this moment concerned. We are concerned with God's revelation about God. If he were not the fountain of revelation about himself, we should have no sure ground for saying anything about him which is definite and concrete. Without him, all our sources of information would be problematic in origin and vague in message. There would be plenty of ground for speculation and conjecture and the posing of innumerable questions, but speculation, conjecture and questioning would be all that we had. There are no conclusive arguments for the existence of God; there are no demonstrative proofs of his character and the nature of his activity.

The Christian faith asserts that God has revealed himself, and shown to men all that men can comprehend about his nature, his activity and his purposes. That this is so is also not a proposition that can be demonstrated. All attempts to avoid this unpleasant (unpleasant, that is, for Christians) fact by interposing doctrines of the infallibility of Church, Pope, Bible or 'Inner Light' have finally broken down.[48] It is an article of *faith,* not of knowledge, that God has revealed himself. Knowledge in this sphere is impossible, since the frontiers of reason have been crossed. Faith alone can cross these frontiers; and we speak of faith as that commitment of our whole selves to the person of Christ, not at any point contrary to reason, but transcending reason, of which the New Testament is full. Such faith in Christ carries with it the faith-conviction that God has revealed himself in Christ — and has done so definitively.

When we say 'Christ' we do not merely mean the 'Jesus of history', the historical personality who lived in Palestine for thirty years and a little more at the end of the first century B.C. and the beginning of the first century A.D., and was 'crucified under Pontius Pilate'. We do mean him, but we also mean the 'Christ of faith', who is the same person as Jesus of Nazareth, seen for what he also is by the eye of faith — Jesus dying for our salvation and the salvation of the whole world, Jesus raised up by God, Jesus ascended into heaven, Jesus alive in the Church which is his body and in all those who love him, Jesus who will come to be our judge. (When we use the words 'raised up', 'ascended', 'alive', 'judge', we do not imply any particular interpretation, literal or other, of the Resurrection, the Ascension and the Parousia; we do imply the doctrines of faith which underlie the interpretations.)

We learn, then, by faith in Christ, thus understood, that God reveals himself in Christ. This is immensely important for theology and ethics and the philosophy of religion. But we also learn much more. We learn that God is the creator of the whole universe; that he is also its sovereign. We learn that he is the source of love and truth and beauty. We learn that he loves, with equal and particular love, every member of his creation; that, in his love for all men, he has willed that they should each reach maturity, wholeness and perfect goodness, according to their God-given faculties and gifts; that, nevertheless, he gives freedom to each and all to accept or reject his love and his purposes; that in the predicament of the human race into which it was led by the bizarre exercise of this freedom, he gave himself to man in the person of Jesus Christ and in him suffered the extremity of injustice and rejection; that the agony and cruelty of the Cross did not destroy or reduce or temper his love for man, so that Christ, having truly died, truly came alive again by the power of the divine love, and lives for ever as the friend and judge and champion of mankind; that the Spirit, who is God

76

active in history and in the Church of Jesus Christ, guides men, as they are able and willing to be guided, into the fullness of the truth as the truth was embodied in Jesus. And also much more that 'neither tongue nor pen can show'.

So far there would be very general agreement among Christians about the content of the revelation in Christ. Now we come to an element in that revelation which may indeed be disputed, but of which it is more accurate to say that it has been overlaid by less-than-Christian considerations and then largely forgotten. In New Testament teaching, that is in the Gospels (though not unequivocally in Matthew), in the Pauline body of teaching, and in the Johannine writings, and also largely, though not without exception, in the other books, the motive for Christian living and conduct is proclaimed to be twofold: the nature and character of God himself and gratitude to God for what he has done and is doing for the welfare of mankind.

The nature and character of God appear already in the Old Testament as the motive for human goodness: 'You shall be holy, because I, the Lord your God, am holy. You shall revere, every man of you, his mother and his father. You shall keep my sabbaths. I am the Lord your God'.[49] Holiness is no doubt there meant in a mostly numinous, only partly ethical sense; but the germ of the idea is present. The notion of obedience to God and of submitting to his laws is, however, in the end much more prominent in the Old Testament, and it is only in the teaching of Jesus that the imitation of God comes fully into the central place which it occupies — or should occupy — in Christian ethics: 'What I tell you is this: Love your enemies and pray for your persecutors; only so can you be children of your heavenly Father, who makes his sun rise on good and bad alike, and sends the rain on the honest and the dishonest. There must be no limit to your goodness, as your heavenly Father's goodness knows no bounds (literally: you shall be perfect, as your heavenly Father is perfect)'.[50]

The true interpretation of this passage has often been obscured by a misunderstanding of the words 'children of your heavenly Father', which have been taken to mean 'sons of God by adoption' in the Pauline sense. The words, in fact, mean, as is clear from the modern study of the language and ideas of Jesus, 'like God', and 'like God' in a deep and inner sense, as the Jews always believed a father and son to be like each other. The Gospel of Matthew in which the phrase occurs has also helped to obscure this point, since, in spite of many sayings and deeds of Jesus in the same sense, which it could not but record, it seeks to cast its whole account of the teaching of Jesus into the framework of a 'new law' to replace the Pentateuch; this is understandable enough when we remember the evangelist's keen desire to persuade Jews and Jewish Christians that Jesus was both the Jewish Messiah and the 'prophet greater than Moses', but it has proved to be very misleading to later generations. Yet the intention of Jesus can now be seen to be perfectly clear.

The author of Ephesians, Paul or one of his disciples, had clearly grasped this: 'In a word, as God's dear children, try to be like him, and live in love as Christ loved you, and gave himself up on your behalf'.[51] And when Paul urges the Corinthians[52] and the Philippians[53] to take him, Paul, as an example, we are not to interpret this in an egotistic sense

78

(though we may have our doubts about the wisdom of this kind of expression), but as amplified implicitly by what Paul says explicitly in a later passage of the First Letter to Corinth: 'Follow my example, as I follow Christ's'.[54] It should be noted, moreover, lest the word 'example' leads us to think that these passages refer to 'the example of Christ' in the manner dear to several generations of liberal theologians, preachers and Sunday School teachers, i.e. 'doing what Christ would have done if he had been here', that a more literal translation would be: Be imitators of me (as I am of Christ), i.e. be *like* me (as I am like Christ).

'Love one another; as I have loved you, so you are to love one another'[55] is the Fourth Gospel's intensification of the same idea. 'There is no greater love than this, that a man should lay down his life for his friends. You are my friends, if you do what I command you'[56] carries the same message. Whatever else of truth is contained in this well-loved passage, and however useful it may be for pointing the message of Remembrance Sunday, its primary meaning is: 'I am about to give up my life for you who are my friends; I call on you to show the same love for your friends, for there is no greater love than this'. And then again, making the same point, we have the First Letter of John: 'It is by this that we know what love is: that Christ laid down his life for us. And we in our turn are bound to lay down our lives for our brothers'.[57] And more profoundly still: 'God is love; he who dwells in love is dwelling in God and God in him';[58] and: 'Everyone who loves is a child of God and knows God; but the unloving know nothing of God. For God is love'.[59]

We can state this motive for goodness in stricter

and more formal terms by saying: the nature of God, who is the ultimate reality (or, as some would say, Being itself) is goodness. Therefore the universe is created and controlled in the interests of goodness, that is, as Christians and others would say, of love. Those who wish to live in the universe in conformity with its ultimate principles will seek to live the good life, or (as Christians and others would put it) the life of love. Jesus and his contemporaries put the same thing more simply.

However it is put, it is a very far cry from the way in which non-Christians usually suppose that Christians conceive ethical motivation; and from the way in which Christians often deform their faith by conceiving it themselves. This mistaken way of conceiving it starts from the idea of commandment. It has to be conceded that the Fourth Gospel uses the word 'commandment' in the very passages quoted above in which it commends the imitation of God: 'This is my commandment: love one another'.[60] 'If you heed my commands, you will dwell in my love'.[61] And Jesus, of course, describes the instructions to love God and to love our neighbour as 'commandments'. What Christian teachers for so long failed to notice, however, or failed to take seriously, is the fact that love cannot be commanded, and that Jesus, surely, knew this. What he is doing, what the Fourth Gospel and the First Letter of John are doing, is to change the very meaning of the word 'commandment' by the paradoxical way in which they use it. 'I command you to love, as God loves' means: 'Others in the name of God have given you laws to obey and commandments to keep; the only 'law', the only 'new commandment' that I give you is: love, as God loves. That's all there is to it'. And if that is all there is to it — and it is in fact a new world altogether — the concept of obeying a command fades out of existence.

If this is not understood, and the words relating to commandments in the Gospels are given their usual significance, the way is open for building ethical systems on a revised form of the Ten Commandments and calling them Christian. God becomes the Supreme Legislator, Jesus is the Rabbi to end all Rabbis, and the Christian life is the keeping of innumerable laws.

One reason for the recurrent degeneration of Christianity into legalism is that when we hear the words: 'Love, as God loves', we immediately feel ourselves to be confronted with an impossible ideal, and, having acknowledged its immense nobility, we sink gratefully into the observance of the many regulations which Christian tradition has worked out for us, revising them from time to time under the pressure of new situations, but seeking always to retain their leading elements. And when we hear the often-quoted (but difficult to track down) aphorism of Augustine 'Love, and do what you like', we are uplifted for the moment, and shortly afterwards return to acting as before.

But the New Testament is not so unrealistic as in our hearts we sometimes suspect it of being. There is another side to ethical motivation as it is there set out. If one side is the vision of God, which in most of us is sadly incomplete and scarcely moves us to action, except at a few high moments of our experience, the other side is simple gratitude for his goodness to us and to all mankind. 'We love, because he loved us first'.[62] This theme of gratitude comes out most clearly, so far as the Gospels are concerned, in the narrative of the dinner party at the home of Simon the Pharisee (and, of course, the evangelist

81

wants us to note that it was at the house of a Pharisee that this happened), when the prostitute came in, uninvited, and washed the feet of Jesus; and Jesus countered the self-righteous horror of his fellow guests by telling the story of the moneylender who, rather surprisingly, let off two of his debtors, one with a large debt, one with a small one. His host and his fellow-guests agreed with the proposition that the debtor with the larger debt would love his indulgent creditor more than the other one would; and Jesus concluded: 'I tell you, the great love of this woman proves that her many sins have been forgiven: where little has been forgiven, little love is shown'.[63]

It is Paul who brings out the full force of this. This he was able to do because he was looking back, not only on the teaching of Jesus about the love of God, but also on the manifestation and embodiment of that love, leading inexorably to self-sacrifice, in Jesus himself. In his letters he brings it out in a way which indicates that the motive of gratitude had been so well taught and learned, at least in the Pauline churches, that it could be taken for granted and built on immediately. In several letters he declares the message which the situation requires, and answers the questions which his friends have put, about the work of God in effecting the forgiveness of sins through Jesus Christ, and cognate matters; and having done this, he proceeds, by the simple insertion of 'therefore', or 'then', to say what kind of life gratitude for God's benefits to us impels us to live. In *Romans* for instance, after the massive exposition of the justifying grace of God, and of his inscrutable wisdom shown in his treatment of the Jewish nation, he first bursts out into a paean of praise: 'O depth of wealth, wisdom, and knowledge in God! How unsearchable his judgements, how untraceable his ways! Source, Guide, and Goal of all that is — to him be glory for ever! Amen.' And he then continues: 'Therefore, my brothers, I implore you by God's mercy to offer your very selves to him'.[64]

The Christian ethic, then, is an ethic of emulation of God, and of gratitude to him, and the two sides of it often slide into one another in Christian writings. Obedience to law, divine or human, or to conscience is not, of course, discounted; but it is secondary, something to fall back upon when the springs of gratitude dry up. To do our duty is admirable; to obey the law of God is admirable; to keep the commandments of the Gospel is admirable. And sometimes these make up all that the best Christian, in his weakness, can do. But the essentially Christian motivation is deeper than any of these things.

The application of this to education is obvious enough. The nature of God, as Christ manifests it, requires us to teach. He teaches at all times — by the revelation which he gives to mankind. He imparts the knowledge of himself and of his word incessantly. He does so, not 'for his name's sake' or 'for his glory' (as the Old Testament often, misleadingly, suggests) but because he is love; and love always gives itself, in the manner appropriate to the occasion and to the person or persons involved. If we are to be in conformity with his purposes for the universe and his attitude to mankind, we also are to teach, if we have the ability so to do.

The education of mankind is part of his purpose for the universe, part of his 'salvation'. Teachers, then, who teach as he teaches, or shall we say, as Christ taught, are fulfilling a role within the design of salvation; and do so, whether they acknowledge the origin or existence of that design or not. Preachers and priests and teachers can be distinguished as three classes of people with a divine vocation. But their functions often converge and overlap, because they are within the same unitary purpose of God. It is for our convenience that we divide them up and train them and employ them differently — just as other human agents of God's salvation are trained and employed differently — though whether we should do this without variation is an open question.

God teaches and reveals, and loves and saves, in a personal and non-coercive fashion. He is gentle: he exercises his immense power to build up and not to destroy; to persuade and not to compel. He teaches in reverence for personality and never in contempt of it or disregard for it. His gift of freedom is never revoked, even when it is scandalously and obdurately misused. For a teacher to imitate God is to be gentle and patient (though not meek and yielding) in the same way, respecting and protecting each man's freedom to his last gasp, working not for his own prestige, credit or promotion, but always for those he teaches, who are not means to an end, however noble, in the mind of the teacher, but ends in themselves.

And when these lofty ideals wither and fade in the presence of the ill-mannered, contra-suggestive, exhibitionist, delinquent offspring of the privileged or non-privileged classes, he continues relentlessly (though probably not imperturbably), because he knows that though he is himself well-brought-up, well-mannered, and orderly in disposition, character and activity, he also needs and has received the infinite patience and mercy of God, and probably of his parents, friends and family also. He is grateful for this, and carries on.

5

Non-Christian Motives

The last few paragraphs of the preceding chapter should not be taken to mean that Christian teachers are ethically superior to those who are not Christians. It could well be in many, or even most cases, that non-Christian teachers achieve a level of devotion to their task and to their pupils' interests which is not equalled by their Christian colleagues. Certainly among the great educationalists of recent decades (earlier decades and centuries are a different matter altogether) — 'great' in the sense that they clearly saw and persuasively enunciated valid and progressive ideals and principles of education — there is no preponderance of Christians; in fact, at certain times the opposite has been true.

Certainly also, if one were to take a sample of a hundred schools of different types and for different age-groups, and investigate the convictions of the teachers in those schools (fortunately such an enterprise is not feasible), there is no reason to expect that in the resulting analysis the teachers who were Christians would turn out always to be the 'good' teachers, in the sense of being ethically motivated to the highest degree. There would be cynics and clock-watchers among the Christians as well as among the others, and men and women who spent

A Christian Theology of Education

many hours for their pupils not required by the time-
table or the conditions of their employment — men
and women who are the real backbone of any school —
would be found in both Christian and non-Christian
groups. And the same result would be reached if
there were to be a survey of heads of schools. This is
true in spite of the fact that the proportion of Christians to non-Christians is higher in the teaching
profession, probably, than in any others (except, of
course the ordained ministry).

It may well be that certain sorts of Christian
conviction lead actually to a lower type of motivation
than that found among non-Christian humanists.
There are several interpretations of the Christian
Gospel which impel those who favour them to regard
everyone they meet as a fit object for immediate
evangelization, the young as well as the mature.
Looking at their pupils (to say nothing of their
colleagues) in this light normally goes along with
a full and accurate knowledge of certain parts of the
Bible, and is likely to produce great devotion to the
task of teaching, as a useful means to their evangelistic end, and a powerful interest in those they teach;
and these qualities are easily mistaken for Christian
motives. It is one of the contentions of this book that
the devotees we have in mind imperfectly understand
the true character of Christian motivation through
the narrowness of their theology. They claim Biblical
authority for their concept of man as possessing a
soul which urgently needs to be saved and of God's
salvation as being concerned only with that soul;
and such Biblical authority is, as we have seen,
lacking. Other Christians would be wrong, and
narrow in their turn, to deny their Christian motivation altogether, but are entitled to say that it is

defective in important respects, and ethically inferior to the best humanistic motives. But for the purposes of our present discussion we do best to eliminate the set of convictions we have just described from the comparison between Christian and non-Christian motives, both in their content and in their effect, and simply say that Christians and non-Christians cannot claim to be ethically superior to each other.

But in spite of the obvious and genuine high-mindedness of many non-Christian educationalists and teachers, stringent and critical questions need to be asked about the motivation which they champion and exemplify. The phrase 'non-Christian' is, of course, far too wide for careful discussion; and there is no great advantage in trying to take into account all the varieties of non-Christian thought. Apart from the educational concepts of the other religions now firmly established in Britain — some of which, no doubt, have something in common with Christian theology, but which, apart from Judaism, cannot yet be discussed with full knowledge — the most substantial non-Christian point of view on the matter can, with all its variations, be described as 'humanist'. Many Christians wish to be called Christian humanists, and the position taken in this book could, it is to be hoped, be fairly described as a Christian humanist position. But popular usage distinguishes Christians from humanists, and at this point it is prudent to defer to popular usage.

Humanists, then, put forward as the aims of education such things as development in knowledge and understanding; personal autonomy; respect for others and for human dignity; fairness and justice for all, and the abolition of discrimination; the encouragement of freedom of thought and action for individuals and communities; the growth of individual personality in community. They hope that children in schools will come to appreciate and appropriate these values as worthwhile in themselves.

What is the humanist ground for believing in these values? It is a notable fact that P. H. Hirst and R. S. Peters, after an exceedingly careful conceptual analysis of these and other values, are forced to conclude that conceptual analysis does not and cannot answer any questions about their justification. 'How is a person who believes in fairness to answer someone who is a determined advocate of some form of discrimination? What arguments can the lover of liberty advance against the kindly despot who puts more emphasis on the virtues of conformity and obedience?' They mention the argument that certain states of mind, including knowledge and understanding, are 'desirable', and should therefore be promoted and encouraged in education. 'But how do we determine which states are desirable? And why should knowledge and understanding be so favoured as a necessary feature of them?' They conclude that their own analysis of education raises but does not solve this sort of 'moral' question, and they do not proceed to give any answer in their book.[65]

These are the very questions that must be pressed on the humanist. What are the ultimate grounds for belief in freedom, and justice, and the development of personality, as 'worthwhile', as 'values'? The answer is sometimes given in terms of the intuition of moral values which we all in some measure possess. But there is no universal moral intuition that freedom is good, or that the development of personality is worthwhile; 'You are nothing, your people is every-thing' was the legend inscribed above the gateway to

German work-camps (not concentration camps, but camps where each German young man and woman was expected to spend some months in helping his nation) in the Nazi period, and Nazism as a politico-ethical system of ideas is not dead. And, so far as justice is concerned, it means so many different things to so many different people, as Plato's *Republic* showed long ago, that the claim to be in favour of justice is a vacuous boast. If we do not know what it is, how can we give convincing grounds for it?

An attempt to answer these questions may be made in the terms of a general moral theory such as utilitarianism. 'The greatest good of the greatest number', it is argued, is plainly promoted if children are brought up to be just and free and independent and co-operative, to respect other people, and to acquire such knowledge and understanding as their abilities allow. But how is 'the greatest good of the greatest number' determined, and by whom? What does 'good' mean in this connection — is it, for instance, moral virtue or happiness? And does 'the greatest number' include all men of every race, or only my fellow-citizens, and perhaps my allies? And, in the last resort, why *should* I serve the greatest good of the greatest number, if it suits my personal interests and welfare to do something which conflicts with the general interest — so long as I get away with it, and perhaps deceive other people into thinking that I am altruistic when I am in fact plain selfish? Why should I be altruistic?

The last questions cannot be satisfactorily answered by saying that unless I and others are at least partially altruistic, society will crumble and disappear. In any case such an answer is not a moral but an expedient one, and it is easily met by the reply: why should

I care if society does crumble and disappear? In other words, the answer only leads us back to the original question. And if we try to answer the original question this time by saying that the moral sense of humanity requires us to think of others, we shall hear the answer, 'Does it? and if it does, why should I obey it?' We have not advanced an inch from Square One.

The Christian comment, then, on humanist motives in education is not that these are not high and highly admirable, but that they are based on inadequate logic. If you grant that the welfare of the human race imposes obligations on every member of it, the rest follows, and we have a series of valid motives for educational actions. But if this is questioned, as it always is by some members of every community, and as it is legitimately open to question by all who reflect deeply on these matters, we look in vain for a convincing answer.

It may, of course, be said, in spite of the argument of the preceding chapter, that Christian motives have no adequate justification either. But they have. Admittedly they depend on, and are part of, the total Christian view of the universe, and stand or fall with this. But this is a view which can stand up to logical criticism; whereas, if the Christian view falls, and Christian motives with it, we are left with a set of motives which have to stand on their own feet with no support from any coherent view of the universe – a very vulnerable position indeed.

What is vulnerable in logic becomes in due course precarious in practice. It sounds like, and is, a Christian cliché that humanists are living on the declining capital of Christian theology. But it is a cliché which cannot be lightly dismissed. The values commended by humanists are the values which flow from Christian theology. Christian theologians and Christian teachers have, historically, derived other and sometimes contradictory values from their theology, but their mistakes have now been exposed, often by humanists, and it is the *true* implications of Christian theology that are now in the open field. But how long can these values survive as living and operative forces in education or anywhere else after their logical basis has been discarded and nothing else has been put in its place?

Some would say that the term of this survival has already been set, and that education, like other civilized activities, is already launched on a steep decline. It is said to be slipping into a barren emphasis on technical expertise, to be concentrating on the short term aim of examination ingenuity, and to have no interest in the development of the imagination, or in real people. The evidence for this is not lacking, but it is still possible to point to counter-balancing factors. The real danger is more serious, far-reaching and insidious: that society as constituted at this particular time in history will take over the educational system, continue to use the old names and profess to further the old values, and in fact insinuate the aims which it wishes to further in the interests of its own survival, calling them 'freedom' and 'individual development' and 'community sense', and really meaning something quite different.

This process is already at work, and it is at this point that the devastating attack by Ivan Illich strikes home. It is easy to blunt the force of his remarks by saying that they are addressed to Puerto Rico (where they began to be uttered), or New York (which provided much of his material), or Mexico (where he conducts his Centre for Inter-cultural Documentation); or by condemning him for over-statement and for misunderstanding what happens in ordinary, decent societies (like Britain, as we should say), because of what happens in other less enlightened places. He *does* have American society in mind, he does exaggerate; and he does propose remedies which are apparently quite unrealistic. But there is enough truth about British bourgeois industrial society in what he says for him to be taken very seriously as the leading critic of present educational practice.

His contention is that in modern society the school has taken over the place once occupied by the Church. The Church used to impose its ideals and ideas on the educational system, with results good and bad which it is easy to see. It has now been displaced by the school. But the school is not the agent of pure learning and the disinterested quest for truth and self-development which it often makes itself out to be. On the contrary, it is the creature of those who have industrialized society and intend to direct its future in accordance with their own self-centred aims, and need a large mass of 'educated' and 'semi-educated' technicians and workpeople if they are to achieve this effect. To this end they have propagated certain 'myths': the myth of 'unending consumption' — that industrial activity always produces something valuable, that the objects produced create demand, and that the demand creates production, and that this process is without qualification *good;* the myth of 'quantified values' — that everything is measurable, including personality and human achievement, and goodness itself: and the myth of 'self-perpetuating progress through the endless accumulation of money and all other kinds of material wealth'. For the propagation of these myths the schools and colleges are the obvious means, and they have therefore been secretly taken over for the purpose. Those who teach in them partly believe in the myths themselves, for they have been conditioned to them by their own training, and those who do not believe in them or have doubts about them are lulled into a false sense of security by the high-sounding words which are used on Speech Days and other ceremonial occasions. 'Only if we understand the school-system as the central myth-making ritual of industrial societies can we explain the deep need for it, the complex myth surrounding it, and the inextricable way in which schooling is tied into the self-image of contemporary man', says Illich in *The Celebration of Awareness*.[66] Using another metaphor, he says that the school is the 'sacred cow' of modern society; and, more elaborately, 'schools indoctrinate the child into the acceptance of the political system his teachers represent, despite the claim that teaching is non-political'.[67]

He also develops the theme in several places that schools induct children into a society which demands specialization and is committed to the dubious ideology of economic growth.[68]

Illich's own remedy for these universal ills is the 'de-schooling of society' in the interests of education. He would obliterate the educational institutions of our culture, with their proud, inbuilt traditions and their guaranteed wealth; and put education back where it belongs, in the family and the local community, free from state manipulation. There is a short but searching critique of Illich's views by J. Stuart Maclure in the *Proceedings of the 12th World Methodist Conference*.[69]

He is for revolution, not reform. We may think that the educational situation in the West has not reached the abysmal depths that Illich describes, and that in the developing countries some considerable knowledge of industrial techniques must be imparted to a large number of people if the countries are to survive, let alone reach a proper standard of life for all their people. But it remains true that education is never conducted, or conducted with any enthusiasm or effect, in an ideological vacuum. If the set of ideas by which it is at one time permeated is discredited and exiled by the next generation, other ruling ideas will take its place, openly or covertly. If it is replied that it is surely possible to run a school on completely 'open' lines (as, presumably, A. S. Neill consistently tried to do) without any suggestion that any idea or value is in itself preferable to any other, the answer to the reply is that the notion that schools should be conducted on open lines is itself ideological. What is in danger of happening in our society, and is beginning to happen, is that under cover of the high ideals in which many heads and their assistants believe, and of the still-maintained inclusion of worship and religious instruction in the syllabus, pure materialism is taking over, fuelled by the monotonous stress laid on the making of money and on material comfort by the mass media, the advertising industry and the structure of commerce and industry. This, then, is the result of the decline of Christian motivation, if the Christian view is correct.

Against this process Christians and humanists have, fortunately, a common cause to make. Christians regard humanist motives and ideas for education as admirable but insecurely based. Humanists regard the basis of good education as stated by Christians as intellectually unsound. But there is enough similarity between the methods which Christians employ and the results which they wish to produce for useful co-operation to be possible. And if it is possible, it is urgently necessary.

Humanists may be disposed to fear that the alleged dogmatism of Christianity makes such co-operation impossible, or, at best precarious, and it may be that the arrogance of some Christians, and the way in which confessional schools have been run, lend colour to this fear. It is by no means certain, for instance, that the liberalization of Roman Catholicism has gone far enough in all areas for full co-operation to be possible, though this is on the way. Yet, in the hope that dogmatism is a thing of the past in Christian educational circles, and the further hope that humanists do not accept the dogmatism of the National Secular Society, we have to ask, from the Christian point of view, if any sacrifice of principle is involved by humanist-Christian co-operation on the basis of the principles which they hold in common. Such co-operation already takes place on many Local Education Committees, on many Governing Bodies, and on many school staffs; but sometimes there is slight discomfort in the minds of those who are committed to one point of view or the other, and it is desirable, if it is possible, to remove this discomfort.

This can be done on grounds of Christian theology. It has already been shown that the educational enterprise, when it is aimed at the development of persons in community and is devoted to the free pursuit and communication of knowledge, is part of God's purpose of salvation. In the abstract, good teachers who are aware that they are taking part in God's purpose of salvation by being teachers are better teachers by reason of this fact. In practice, so many other factors are included in the concept of a 'good' teacher that this tends to remain a merely abstract truth.

More to the point is the doctrine of the Holy Spirit, God active in human affairs to further his purpose of salvation by love and persuasion. Some 'sectarian' forms of Christianity have alleged that the Holy Spirit co-operates with and guides and empowers only those who have a specifically Christian faith, so that he is wholly absent from campaigns for liberation, or universal education, or the relief of suffering, except that he 'indwells' those individual Christians who take part in these activities. But this is tantamount to saying that he does not enter human life unless he has a formal invitation — a human attitude, surely, rather than a divine one. It is a feature of the modern charismatic movement in some of its forms that it tends to limit the activity of the Holy Spirit, virtually if not officially, to his 'extraordinary' manifestations in speaking with tongues or spiritual healing. Who, then, it may be asked, is responsible for growth in character and the development of Christian qualities and the exploration of Christian truth? Surely the Holy Spirit, if the New Testament is to be trusted.

The Holy Spirit himself is not subject to the limitations which some of his recipients try to impose on him. He is for ever active, not only in the Church, where he has the specific tasks of binding Christians together, guiding them more fully into the truth as it is found in Jesus Christ, and making real and contemporary through the Sacraments the action of Jesus Christ in forgiveness and reconciliation; but he is active also in human society, wherever men pursue

96

aims which are part of God's purpose for mankind, under whatever flag they do so and with whatever philosophy, or absence of philosophy, they undergird their actions. The Holy Spirit is the Spirit sent by Christ, who said both 'he who is not with me is against me'[70] (for all responsible people must take sides for good or evil) and also 'he who is not against us is on our side'[71] (for many who visited the sick and the prisoner, and clothed the naked did not know that they were thus serving Christ and were surprised to be told so[72]). Since both Christians and non-Christians are guided by the Holy Spirit, and their work is furthered by him, they can surely work together.

In speaking of 'non-Christians' we have so far, with good reason, concentrated on the humanists, and we have noted that it is very difficult as yet to include the motives of non-Christian religions in our survey, with the partial exception of Judaism. So far as Judaism is concerned, it would seem that exponents of that faith are just as inclined as Christians to find a religious foundation for education, and to find it in the Torah, as the Law given by God to man, and including not only the ethical sections of the Old Testament, but also the whole teaching about man's relation to God and to his fellows which the Rabbis have accumulated in their commentaries on Holy Writ. How far the same appeal would be made to the Law of God in this matter by Muslims, Hindus, Sikhs and Buddhists, or what other religious motivation they would adduce, must be left to the teachers of these various faiths to expound. Here it may be useful, as a kind of filling out of this chapter, to suggest the possible grounds for co-operation between Christians and the adherents of non-Christian faiths

97

which may soon be required in this country by the march of events, and already happens with the Jewish community, by stating theologically the relationship between Christianity and non-Christian religions.

This is more easily offered, unfortunately, than provided. For within Christendom itself there are divisions of thought which go right back into the New Testament. The Jews are, of course, from the beginning a special case. In the New Testament they are both the people to whom God has revealed his will and made his promises, and the murderers of Christ and the persecutors of his Church. So Paul laments their apostasy, but is assured that one day they will regain their rightful place in God's kingdom, and that all Israel will be saved. John reminds his readers that salvation is of the Jews and proceeds to describe them as the vexatious and relentless enemies of Jesus and his followers. This ambiguity pursues them through history. To Christians they have been at one time the divinely chosen precursors of the Gospel; at another deicidal miscreants whose main aim is to subvert the very foundations of Christianity. It is not necessary to show how grievously the Jews have suffered from this ambiguity. But now that all Christian Churches have at last dropped the charge of deicide, of which many Christians were unaware until it was about to be dropped, surely we can put a high value on Jewish aims and motives in education and work with them over a large area of educational practice.

We come to a yet more difficult problem. Jesus refused to condemn a man who was driving out devils in a name other than his.[73] Paul at Athens claimed that 'pagans' worshipped the true God in ignorance, and dispersed that ignorance by speaking of Jesus as the fulfilment of what they had imperfectly grasped.[74] John describes the Word of God, who is Jesus, as the light which lightens every man by coming into the world.[75] But Paul also describes the worship of pagans in highly unflattering terms,[76] and John denies that anyone can come to the Father except through Jesus Christ. (This *can* be taken to mean that only through Jesus can God be known as *Father,* though his other attributes can be known in other ways.)[77]

After this awkward beginning the Christian Church has never quite known what to make of other faiths. To Justin and Clement in the early centuries, their representatives, or at least the best of them, could be called 'Christians before Christ'; but Tertullian dismissed the same people as worshippers of demons and blasphemous seducers of the faithful. On the whole, it is the exclusive views of Tertullian which prevailed until the modern world so completely mixed up races and religions in its metropolitan centres that Christians have had to think about the whole problem again.

They are still undecided, as is shown by the continuing dispute whether services of other faiths can be held in Christian Churches even when the adherents of those faiths have nowhere else where they can worship. Does the fact that worship is offered to God through Jesus Christ by the use of Christian symbols and liturgy in a particular building rule out the possibility that worship to God may be offered under the forms of another religion in which Christ has no place, or only a subordinate place, in that building? Some Christians say 'Yes', some 'No'; some even suggest that Muslims and others worship a different

God from the God of the Christians; some, at the other extreme, urge that so long as God is worshipped, the exact forms and names and rites and symbols matter very little, though they themselves prefer the Christian ones.

This shows widespread confusion. Few Christians now wish to exclude the study of 'other religions' from the syllabus of schools in a 'Christian' country; comparative religion is *in,* though it had to fight hard for its place. And soon the question will have to be faced: when the request comes for a course in Islamic culture, or in Black Studies, or in Indian civilization, to be included in school curricula in certain areas of the country, what is the Christian attitude to be? If it were to happen that the Sikh Community, or the Muslim Community, in Birmingham or Bradford, say, were to ask for help in maintaining its own school, should such a request be supported and assisted by Christians?

The theological position outlined in this book suggests an affirmative answer, however great will be the misgivings of some. There is, first of all to be taken into account, the traditional (but often questioned) conviction that 'other religions' are fulfilled in Christ; that in his person, work and teaching, he takes up and transcends all that is true and good in other faiths (as he is already believed to have done in respect of Judaism) and corrects anything that may be false. This conviction involves a positive attitude to other religions, as inspired by God and probably containing truths not revealed in Christianity. The doctrine of the Holy Spirit which we have given above readily copes with this belief about the relationship of Christianity to non-Christian faiths.

Second, we have maintained that God's salvation-purpose includes all that tends in the direction of human maturity, understanding and goodness. Christians are naturally a little surprised by certain elements in the belief and practice of other religions, and tend to dwell on them as indicating the superiority of Christianity. But this is unseemly, especially when Hindus and Muslims and others can easily point out elements in Christian faith and worship, and what is alleged to be Christian practice, which are at odds with Christian principles and professions, and indeed with those of the other 'high religions' of the world. We are in duty bound to judge other religions by the best that they contain, as we hope to be judged ourselves, and it is almost patronizing, though undoubtedly correct, to say that the best in the religions of which we speak promote human maturity, understanding and goodness — far more so than many of the secularisms and materialisms of our time which have free rein in our schools.

In the last analysis, then, the issues just considered are in principle the same as those which come under the heading of 'humanist motives', and the theological answer turns out to be much the same also.

And the conclusion is also the same for humanists and for other non-Christians in respect of the educational safeguards which educationalists will wish to enact. The cry of 'indoctrination' rises loud and clear when any group of people known to have definite religious or political views is (as it is put) 'let loose' in the classroom, though it is curiously muted when made up of rationalists or materialists (perhaps because they are mostly not organized in groups, but simply permeate society). The cry, in spite of its occasional shrillness, is a cry for justice and must be

101

heeded. Christians have, at last, as much under the pressure of public opinion as by the application of Christian theology (which should have been the reason), virtually dropped the attempt to indoctrinate in the classroom. The same restriction needs to be accepted by other committed people, whether they be materialists, humanists, or adherents of non-Christian religions. With these reservations in mind we may look forward to a time when, in our increasingly multi-racial, multi-religious society, the teachers of various faiths will agree together that education needs a foundation in religion, disagree as to which religion is best suited to the purpose, but work together to a growing extent on the principles which they have in common.

6

Practical Consequences

A theology which has no practical consequences is worth nothing at all. Theology has often been pursued as a purely abstract science, and those who have so pursued it have felt no obligation to show how it applies to the actual life lived by men and women in the conditions of the time, still less to make the application themselves, comparing themselves, perhaps, with those sociologists who acknowledge no obligation to improve the life of society. But this is to miss the point of Christian theology, and perhaps of the theology of other religions as well. Christian theology is about the relation of God to man at all points of human life, individual and corporate; and since, in the Christian view, man is at all times *coram Deo,* in God's presence, there is no human experience which lies outside the scope of theology, though there may be many which lie outside its present competence. The relation of God to man is personal and dynamic; God by his active love for man is for ever calling for a response from him. When that response is given, it is in the form of worship, prayer, thought, attitudes, words and actions. Human response is part of the God-man relationship, and the response in all its forms, from liturgy to everyday behaviour, is part of the material of theology; and what is done in the world of education is a very important part of that response. Therefore there are consequences for education from Christian theology properly understood.

The practical consequences which seem to follow for education from Christian theology, as we have tried to set it out, are given here in a series of theses, some short, some longer; in some the logical process from what has gone before is fairly obvious, in some it may not be quite so clear, but (it is to be hoped) nevertheless discernible.

(a) The Church has a vital and inescapable interest in all parts of the educational process and in all aspects of educational organisation. This is not to say that it has expertise in all the matters in which it is interested, but the interest must be asserted. Methods of teaching, the training of teachers, the drawing up of curricula, the size of classes and of schools, the selection of pupils, and the financing of the whole complex of matters on a local and a national scale, raise questions on which Christians should exercise a considered judgement when they have mastered the facts: this judgement will, it may be hoped, be frequently the same as that of the majority of educational experts and practitioners — when they agree together — but sometimes it may be different.

This is not staking a claim to take over education again. Such a claim is in any case ludicrous, but even if it were not, it should not now be made. When the Church in fact controlled education, it did so often with conspicuous success, and often also with conspicuous faults. But because of the secularization of society there is no case for the resumption of ecclesiastical control. Yet there are strong reasons why the standpoint or standpoints of the Church on the various issues should first of all be made clear in Christian minds, and then stated and heard in the places where decisions are taken.

To make this difficult, there is much ignorance on the one side, and the sometimes complacent consciousness of knowledge on the other; and prejudice on both. But this can be overcome on both sides if the will is present.

(b) If it is permissible to draw up a 'hierarchy of values' in education, then Christians will put the interests of the child and the student at the top, and those of the teacher second: those of administrators and the Government of the day come low down in the scale. In this sense, as in others, education should be 'child-centred'; the child in whom it is centred is the child as an individual, the child in his family, the child in his social, national, and (as we must unfortunately still say) racial context; the child as he is known about by his parents and teachers, by psychologists and sociologists; and above all, the child as a growing person who has to live in the rapidly changing communities which are characteristic of the modern period.

(c) Nothing matters so much as the child's welfare. But teachers are essential to him. Teachers are, or should be, the most influential members of any community. This was much better recognised by some ancient and medieval cultures, and by some cultures outside the West, than it is by us. The low esteem in which teachers are held may be partly due to their own faults, and partly to the comparative smallness of the salaries they have been able to extract from the Government — and partly to the apparent length of their holidays. But it is much more an indication of the materialistic emphasis of our culture. The achieve-

105

ments of teachers are in the realm of persons — of the mind, the imagination and the will; they do not increase profits or productivity or prestige. Therefore (it is thought) they are of small account.

But to the Christian they are the transmitters of culture and wisdom and knowledge; and they are the first and most effective interpreters of life to each succeeding generation. They specialize in the field of personal relations, and they are persons themselves. Therefore their training and their conditions of life, and their opportunities for developing their techniques and increasing their knowledge are second only in importance to the welfare of those whom they teach.

(d) A further major concern of the Church is the *recruitment* of teachers. The policy of the Department of Education and Science does not need any longer to be 'as many teachers as possible in the shortest possible time', and we may hope that it will never become so again, even though the Government's estimate of the teachers required by 1981 as 510,000[78] is thought by many to be unduly small, in view of the intolerable size of classes in many areas. Presumably now it is possible to concentrate on recruiting and training teachers of the highest calibre, and, if such persons need honourable incentives in greater numbers and with greater force, then these incentives should be provided. Good teachers belong to many different types of religious and non-religious convictions; they have in common an interest in children and other students as persons. The Church is an important agent, from its own point of view, and from the point of view of all educational authorities, for the recruitment of people who have the necessary qualities to become good teachers. It is not necessary to add that this refers to teachers of every subject in every kind of institution.

(e) There is still an important place in the educational system for confessional schools and colleges. There is no chance that these will ever again constitute a majority, even in the United States, which has a proliferation of Church-related Liberal Arts Colleges and other places of higher education. Nor is there any good reason to be sorrowful about this. Nor should it be suggested that all teachers who are Christians should be trained in Church colleges and teach in Church schools. This is highly undesirable. But if there are Christian principles of education and if there is a Christian theology of education, then these principles and this theology should be expressed in two ways: one, in the presence on the staff of as many schools and colleges as possible of those who will bring Christian judgements to bear on the whole life of their community; two, in the existence of schools and colleges, teaching-and-learning communities which are organised and maintained with the deliberate purpose, among others, of embodying Christian ideals and judgements — to be examples of what education is when it is conducted in this way.

One minor advantage which accrues from the situation which exists at present, and ought to continue, is that at last in our time Christian institutions are in a position to make it clear that they do not wish to impose adherence to the Christian faith on their members, and believe wholeheartedly in the freedom of each individual to choose his own philosophy of life; and to do this without falling over backwards to show how liberal they are.

(f) The enlightened teaching of the Bible, the Christian Faith, the history of Christianity, the meaning of non-Christian faiths, and the application of faith, Christian and non-Christian, to ethics, economics, politics and social life, is integral to education. The pitch for the discussion of this matter has been long queered by the fact of *compulsory* religious education in the schools of Britain, and the *banishment* of religious education from the schools of America and other countries. There is no longer any need (if there ever was one) for either the compulsion or the banishment; what is needed is the recognition that no child is educated in any valuable sense unless he has been made aware, imaginatively as well as intellectually, of Christianity and other religions as an essential part of the history and present existence of humanity, and as making a claim upon him for allegiance which he must in the end either accept or reject. If anyone is denied the opportunity of gaining that awareness and facing that decision, a gross injustice is done to him, since he is deprived of the knowledge that, as a human being, he is required to pass his own judgement on the basic issues of existence.

The failure of many teachers of religion and ethics (and of many head teachers in all types of school, as they would be the first to admit) to avoid causing this deprivation is evident. It seems that recent improvement in methods of teaching Christianity in schools has done little to arrest the decline, or assist the development, of responsible thought and conduct in the Western countries where it has taken place, though its exact results are not yet known. This is no reason for desisting from what is being done, but a good reason for trying to do it much better.

The claim that 'R.E.' in enlightened form should be regarded as an essential part of any education may look like a disguised version of the old attempt to exercise undue influence on the young by imposing Christianity on them from a privileged position. But it is not. For by 'an enlightened form of R.E.' is meant a much fuller practical recognition than often occurred in the past of the God-given freedom of the pupil. To teach Christianity means nowadays above everything else to show by word and attitude and relationship that in the light of Christ we believe ourselves called to make responsible choices in a world intended and enabled by God to be a community of persons. It is the opposite of indoctrination.

Looked at in this way, the claim on behalf of R.E. is not an infringement of freedom but a demand for freedom. In earlier decades it could be argued by non-Christians with some truth that it was unfair to give children an extra, compulsory dose of religion when they had so much of it already; and sensible Christians anyway were afraid of the counter-productive quality of indoctrination. But now the boot is decidedly on the other foot. Every child is surrounded, from a time not long after his birth, by non-Christian influences of a subtle, pervasive and ultimately almost overwhelming force. The mass-media, the temper of social relationships and cultural life, the popular notion of science, the breakdown of Christian institutions, the decline of Church and Sunday School attendance, the disrepute of Christian morals, all point in his mind with depressing unanimity to the doubtfulness, even the falsity, of Christianity; and no child alive can be impervious to what is being said, whispered, hinted and lived out all around him, even if his own home is comparatively insulated from it. This is a more arrant and constant form of compulsion than compelled religious worship or teaching ever was, even at its worst. To counteract this loss of freedom by educational methods is a blow for liberty.

(g) One powerful cause of the ineffectiveness of R.E. is the extreme difficulty of doing it well. This difficulty is not nearly as widely recognised as it should be, even by teachers themselves. The Bible itself, for all the comfort which the English versions of it give to the uncomplicated, is an extremely hard book to read with full understanding; even the best of us are constantly tempted to read into it what we want to find, or to fall back into old-fashioned fundamentalism in the understanding and acceptance of a text which may have a quite different meaning and possess a quite different authority from that traditionally ascribed to it. Biblical scholarship is a highly sophisticated affair; Christian theology is a complex intellectual exercise. To pass on the inwardness of such a subject, and the duty to reach individual judgements about it, in a very limited time, to children whose other classroom activities are much more direct and practical, is a task fit for heroes and heroines.

Yet the teaching of the way to do it, in spite of recent improvements, is still not in a very advanced condition. It is reassuring to find that 41% of lecturers in R.E. in Colleges of Education feel the aim of their course to be 'to think creatively about the religious education of pupils'. This figure is the result of a questionnaire sent round by a Working Party set up by the British Council of Churches.[79] But it is not so reassuring to find that in actual syllabuses Biblical Studies (very necessary) have a heavy preponderance over other subjects such as modern theology, world religions, and philosophy of religion, which might be thought to be equally important.[80] There is strong evidence, too, for the contention that the provision of professional or method training for specialists is wholly inadequate.[81]

The report just quoted indicated the appalling shortage of qualified teachers of the subject.[82] Even if that could be redressed, no real satisfaction with the situation could be felt until courses were generally available which could result for the men and women being trained in what the following words describe: 'The study of man's search for meaning and his sense of the transcendent will be combined with a sympathetic understanding of the ways in which men have expressed their insight, their hopes and fears, and their wrestling with the problems of freedom and responsibility. So the future teacher will be able to provide his pupils with a sense of perspective on society and history and to encourage a responsible participation in it.'[83]

(h) The organisation of education on a national and local scale is plainly a political matter, since the business of politics is, precisely, the ordering of economic and social life for the public welfare and the benefit of the individual members of the community. But politics, in this proper sense, must be sharply distinguished from party politics, with which it is often confused. Party politics aims at the attainment of political ends by the formation and continuance of parties, whose members agree to work together for the common ends of the party, as being for the most part identical with the political ends which they have accepted for themselves (though they may not be equally enthusiastic about all of them and may indeed repudiate some).

111

In one sense education is a party-political matter as well as a political matter. Each party which seeks to gain the support of the electorate in order to put its principles into effect is rightly expected to have a policy in respect of education (though it is very rare for a party to come to power chiefly on its educational policy). But in another sense it is a party-political matter only to a limited degree. The political parties, as at present constituted, are principally concerned with the use, increase and distribution of the country's resources and the management of the economy, with the maintenance of justice, with the health and general welfare of those who in various degrees need (as we nearly all do) financial assistance and the social services, and with the conduct of foreign affairs and defence. Their programmes in relation to all these matters, except foreign affairs and defence, and to some extent in relation to them also, are mainly based on their theories of economics, social justice and political power (though it is not unknown for pragmatic factors to change the policy of a Government when it is in power from what it offered to the electors in order to gain power).

Education comes in part under the general heading of social welfare and justice, and requires the expenditure of a large amount of the national income (more than it has ever in fact received). So far it will rightly fall to be organised in conformity with the doctrines of the party in power; and the Minister of Education, in particular, will have to fight in the Cabinet for the money that is needed for educational projects, against those ministers, or the Treasury itself, who wish to allocate the money to other purposes.

But large areas of educational policy fall outside

the scope of party politics altogether, and are, in fact, *sui generis*. For instance, it is universally agreed that there should be equal educational opportunities for all; and there is a certain amount of public money available for ensuring this. But the question whether the best way of providing these opportunities with the money available is by a uniform system of comprehensive, co-educational, secondary education, or by a mixture of single-sex and co-educational comprehensive schools, or by a mixture of comprehensive and grammar and technical schools, or by a mixture of independent, direct grant and state-controlled schools (or by some other mixture) cannot be solved by reference to Socialist theories of the nationalization of wealth or to Liberal or Conservative theories of private enterprise. It is a purely educational question and should be solved on educational grounds alone.

This may be distasteful to party leaders, but the recognition of its truth might help them in the management of their parties and the achievement of their party's ends. Socialist leaders would be saved the embarrassment of having Socialists in their ranks who believe in independent grammar school education as an ingredient in the best form of education for some; and Conservative and Liberal leaders the embarrassment of having otherwise loyal supporters who believe in a considerable measure of comprehensive education. During the recent Arab-Israeli war, the Government's policy of an embargo on arms to both sides was submitted to a free vote in the House of Commons. Should not the same method be followed of ascertaining the will of the House on many educational issues, including that of the complete or partial comprehensivization of secondary education? It is nonsensical and disastrous to speak in one breath of child-centred education, and to promise support to it, and in the next to reorganize the education of a city on grounds of party politics alone.

(i) There is a strong Christian case for the kind of diversity in secondary education, and probably in primary education, which already exists in further and higher education. Since the Nazis lost power, no one has seriously suggested that all colleges and universities should be reduced to uniformity, even though so much public money is now spent on them. But in secondary education the tendency to assimilate each to all and all to each is strong, no doubt for the sake of economy and administrative convenience. But the needs of the child are paramount – much more important than a parent's choice in itself, though it is to be hoped that the parent's choice normally corresponds to the needs of the child, as it usually does, except when snobbery enters into the question. Therefore it must first be asked: What kind of educational community does the child or group of children need for its personal development? Since the answer will differ considerably from child to child and from group to group, it follows that we must keep in existence a number of different types of school. We shall need boarding schools and day schools; we shall need grammar schools with the best traditions of the grammar schools and the best public schools; we shall need small comprehensive schools, and larger comprehensive schools; we may need secondary modern schools in an updated form, though this is more doubtful. Shall we need independent schools and direct grant schools? Yes, until the State can afford to provide the kind of education, excellent for some boys and girls, which the best independent and direct grant schools provide; and that day can be prepared for by the progressive entry of children paid for from public funds into the schools in question. At present both independent schools and comprehensive schools are socially divisive. The way forward lies in the penetration of each type of school by the best elements in the other: not in the destruction of either.

What we do not need, but have already got in distressingly large numbers, is enormous comprehensive schools where the most-gifted children receive personal attention for one reason, and the troublesome children receive it for a different one, while the vast mass of children in between, each of them with his own individuality to develop, his own hopes and needs to fulfil, his own fears and problems to cope with, is in grave danger of being totally submerged in the multitude, however carefully the pastoral system of the school is organized. There is no child-centredness in schools of this sort, nor any justice, except the most primitive, for the individual child.

There are many other practical consequences of a sound Christian theology of education. The foregoing ones are surely matters for active discussion, and are sufficient to show in themselves that Christians are serious when they quote St. Paul: 'all that is true, all that is noble, all that is just and pure, all that is lovable and gracious, whatever is excellent and admirable — fill all your thoughts with these things'.[84] The verse could even serve as a summary of the contentions of this book.

REFERENCES

Ref. No.

[1] The text is ROTAS
           OPERA
           TENET
           AREPO
           SATOR

[2] F. H. Bradley: *The Principles of Logic* (Oxford University Press), Vol II, page 591.

[3] See Kenneth Wilson: *Making Sense of it* (Epworth Press), pages 199–205.

[4] 1932 and subsequent years (S.P.C.K.), translated by Philip S. Watson.

[5] Isaiah 55: 8–11.

[6] II Corinthians 4: 6.

[7] Isaiah 55: 6.

[8] Job 23: 3–5.

[9] Job 38–42: 6.

[10] Matthew 7: 7–8.

[11] Acts 17: 26–28.

[12] *Pensées*, section VII, 553.

[13] 1936 (Gollancz).

[14] See page 133 of his book, and the Introduction to the second edition.

[15] *Institutes* I *V* 12.

[16] See J. Macquarrie,*Twentieth Century Religious Thought* (S.C.M.) pp. 324 ff.

[17] Hebrews 11: 6:

[18] Lecture: 'Towards a Theology of Education', *Christian Values in the Boarding School* (Bloxham Research Unit, 15, Norham Gardens, Oxford). See also Part I, 1. of Methodist Commission Report: *Christian Commitment in Education* (Epworth) 1970.

[19] Pp. 91–94.

[20] Ian T. Ramsey, *Christian Values in the Boarding School* pp. 4–17.

[21] *Christian Ethics and Contemporary Philosophy* (S.C.M.) pp. 152–171.

[22] Allen Lane, 1970.

[23] Op. cit. p. 272.

[24] Routledge and Kegan Paul (1970).

[25] Presumably in the purely logical sense.

[26] *Logic of Education* p. 3.

[27] Ovid: *Metamorphoses* VII 20.

[28] Rousseau: *Social Contract* (Everyman Edition) Introduction p. XLI.

[29] *Pity My Simplicity* 1962.

[30] Roland H. Bainton: *Erasmus of Christendom* (Collins) 1969 pp. 227–236.

[31] *Hamlet* II ii 316. The punctuation is, of course, disputed.

[32] *Hamlet* III i 128.

[33] Allen and Unwin, 1972, pp. 39 ff.

[34] A. G. Ives: *Kingswood School in Wesley's Day and Since* (Epworth) pp. 8 ff; cf. p. 75 f.

[35] cf. his *Essay concerning Human Understanding* XVI 4.

[36] For the content of this, see Roland H. Bainton: *Erasmus of Christendom* pp. 86–94.

[37] Isaiah 1: 18; 2 Corinthians 4: 2.

[38] Genesis 2: 7.

[39] Cf. 1 Corinthians 12: 14–26, n.b. v. 20.

[40] For the most concise account of this whole matter, see 'Man' in J. J. Von Allmen's *Vocabulary of the Bible* (Lutterworth) 1958.

[41] Luke 4: 18, 19.

[42] Romans 8: 19–21.

[43] S.C.M., 1974.

[44] See quotations in David Ayerst and A. S. T. Fisher: *Records of Christianity* (O.U.P.) 1971 Vol. I pp. 96 f, 194 f.

[45] M. F. J. McDonnell: *History of St. Paul's School* (Chapman and Hall) 1909, pp. 35–68.

[46] See J. Needham (ed.) *The Teacher of Nations* 1942, which is the fullest account in English of Comenius' ideas and work.

[47] See J. Needham (ed.) *The Teacher of Nations* 1942.

[48] As I have tried to show in my *Religious Authority in an Age of Doubt* (Epworth) 1968.

[49] Leviticus 19: 2, 3.

[50] Matthew 5: 44–48.

[51] Ephesians 5: 1, 2.

[52] 1 Corinthians 4: 16.

[53] Philippians 3: 17.

[54] 1 Corinthians 11: 1.

[55] John 13: 34.

[56] John 15: 13.

[57] 1 John 3: 16.

[58] 1 John 4: 16.

[59] 1 John 4: 7, 8.

[60] John 15: 12.

[61] John 15: 10.

[62] 1 John 4: 19.

[63] Luke 7: 47.

[64] Romans 11: 33–36; 12: 1 cf. 1 Thessalonians 5: 11, Ephesians 4: 1, Colossians 2: 6.
[65] P. H. Hirst and R. S. Peters: *The Logic of Education* pp. 25–41 (especially pp. 39–41).
[66] Calder & Boyars Ltd.
[67] *The Celebration of Awareness* p.119
[68] Ibid. p. 126
[69] Ed. L. F. Tuttle: (Abingdon) 1972 pp. 171 ff.
[70] Matthew 12: 30.
[71] Mark 9: 40.
[72] Matthew 25: 37–39.
[73] Luke 9: 49, 50.
[74] Acts 17: 22–31
[75] John 1: 9.
[76] E.g. in 1 Corinthians 12: 2.
[77] John 14: 6.
[78] White Paper: *A Framework for Expansion* 1972.
[79] *The Recruitment, Employment and Training of Teachers concerned with Religious Education in England and Wales* 1971, p. 23.
[80] Ibid.
[81] Ibid.
[82] Ibid. pp. 8–10
[83] Ibid. p. 25
[84] Philippians 4: 8.